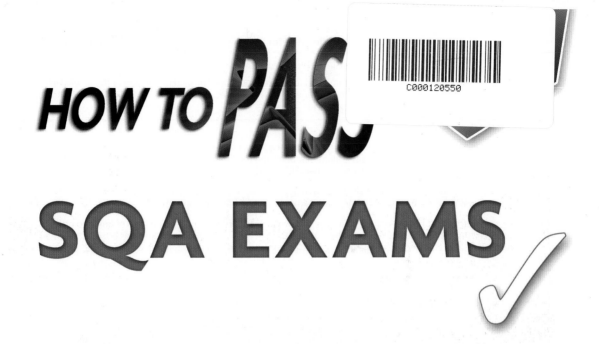

HOW TO PASS

SQA EXAMS

Ian Geddes

**HODDER
GIBSON**

AN HACHETTE UK COMPANY

The Publishers would like to thank the following for permission to reproduce copyright material:

Photo credits

Page 4 Scottish Credit & Qualifications Framework diagram reproduced by kind permission of the SCQF Partnership – www.scqf.org.uk; Page 8 © Hodder Gibson; Page 64 © Thomas Peterson/Alamy; Page 72 © Georgios Kollidas/Alamy; Page 77 © Ashley Coombes/Epicscotland

Acknowledgements

Author: I would like to thank students at Greenwood Academy, Irvine for their support and cooperation in my research for this book. Special thanks to Calum Campbell and the 'boys' from the Geography Department. Finally I would like to thank my wife, Susan Chan, for her advice and for keeping me 'grounded' whilst writing.

Every effort has been made to trace all copyright holders, but if any have been inadvertently overlooked the Publishers will be pleased to make the necessary arrangements at the first opportunity.

Although every effort has been made to ensure that website addresses are correct at time of going to press, Hodder Gibson cannot be held responsible for the content of any website mentioned in this book. It is sometimes possible to find a relocated web page by typing in the address of the home page for a website in the URL window of your browser.

Hachette UK's policy is to use papers that are natural, renewable and recyclable products and made from wood grown in sustainable forests. The logging and manufacturing processes are expected to conform to the environmental regulations of the country of origin.

Orders: please contact Bookpoint Ltd, 130 Milton Park, Abingdon, Oxon OX14 4SB. Telephone: (44) 01235 827720. Fax: (44) 01235 400454. Lines are open 9.00 – 5.00, Monday to Saturday, with a 24-hour message answering service. Visit our website at www.hoddereducation.co.uk. Hodder Gibson can be contacted direct on: Tel: 0141 848 1609; Fax: 0141 889 6315; email: hoddergibson@hodder.co.uk

© Ian Geddes 2010
First published in 2010 by
Hodder Gibson, an imprint of Hodder Education,
An Hachette UK Company
2a Christie Street
Paisley PA1 1NB

Impression number   5 4 3 2 1
Year   2014 2013 2012 2011 2010

Cover photo © Hodder Gibson
Illustrations by DC Graphic Design Limited. Cartoons by Richard Duszczak Cartoon Studio Limited.
Typeset in Frutiger Light 9.5 by DC Graphic Design Limited, Swanley Village, Kent
Printed in Italy

A catalogue record for this title is available from the British Library

ISBN: 978 1444 10839 2

CONTENTS

Preface How to pass exams 1

Introduction The Scottish Qualifications Authority (SQA) 3

Chapter 1 So then, what's this studying game all about? 6

Chapter 2 Some basics 10

Chapter 3 Use your brain! 35

Chapter 4 Your SQA exams – the inside story 52

Chapter 5 Dealing with stress 59

Chapter 6 The exam approaches 67

Appendices Tips for parents 74

Calum's top ten tips for happiness and advancement 78

Exam howlers 81

Useful websites 82

Photocopiable summary sheets 83

HOW TO PASS EXAMS

What do you need to do to be successful in SQA (or, indeed, any) exams? I was once told that passing an exam requires 35 per cent knowledge, 35 per cent luck, 40 per cent knowing how to pass an exam, and – according to my mum – two per cent having a good breakfast! Obviously, that's not good advice for a maths exam…

No two people study in the same way – everyone is different. Motivation is a key factor and, if you are not really bothered or 'up for it', then you may be wasting your time, your life and your future. However, this little book will give you tips and advice to make the most of your skills.

It is not a matter of how hard or how long you study but how SMART you study. This book contains a good deal of common sense and lots of study techniques and tips. In writing this book, I have been assisted by many students who were going through the torment of exams: they have certainly kept me right, and pulled me back from some of the original ideas I had (for example: 'Mr Geddes are you mad? Expecting us to revise without music?').

Studying need not be hard and there are a huge number of 'learning style' systems to be looked up online if you wish to research them. But this book will introduce you to a couple of the basic methods, and you can judge for yourself which one does it for you. Many years ago a book came out entitled, 'Physics is Fun', and I thought about calling this book, 'Sitting Exams is Fun!' Now, when you finish shaking your head in disagreement, think about it for a moment. What I want to do with this book is to give you the skills to do the best that you possibly can. There will be some fun, but I hope there will be little in the way of boredom. I have gone for a 'snappy' approach.

As a learner you have access to vast amounts of information. No other group in history has had the opportunities that you have with computer and mobile-based resources on CD, DVD, MP3, Apps and so on. Fast, wireless internet connections can give you access to huge amounts of information anywhere at any time. Increasingly, you are expected to become an 'independent learner', taking responsibility for what you learn. All this information can be confusing. The more knowledge you have, the more difficult it can be to judge how to use it best. Finding a structure that helps you to process and prioritise all of this information will make studying less confusing.

Remember that there is no 'right' way to study, as long as the method you choose enables you to gain an understanding and a solid grasp of key facts and processes. This way you will be able to study smarter, not harder! Throughout this book I have included some SAQs, or 'Self Assessment Questions'. I have also suggested time for 'Personal Reflection'. Give some thought to these tasks.

At the back of this book you will find a series of summary sheets:

◆ Reading

◆ Taking notes

◆ Time management

◆ Enjoy your learning

◆ Revision techniques

◆ Exam techniques

◆ Weekly study planner

They have been tested by a wide range of my former students, nearly all of whom found them very helpful and effective (although, as you'll learn from the rest of this book, it's all about developing your own style of study). Anyway, if you find these pages helpful, they can be (legally!) photocopied and used as part of your revision strategy.

About the author:

Ian Geddes is a former Deputy Head Teacher at Greenwood Academy, who has recently retired to concentrate on writing, travelling and pursuing his hobby (and business) as a photographer. Ian has marked for SQA at Standard Grade and Higher level, and was commissioned by SQA to write material at Advanced Higher level as well as jointly writing Higher Still assessment material for Intermediate and Higher Geography. Ian is a member the Scottish Association of Geography Teachers and the Royal Scottish Geographical Society. He wrote the first-ever book in Hodder Gibson's award-winning (and SQA endorsed) *How to Pass* series, and we are delighted that he has brought his unique and entertaining style to this book of advice for SQA exam students of every subject.

THE SCOTTISH QUALIFICATIONS AUTHORITY (SQA)

Although this book contains relevant study skills and techniques for any exam, it has been written specifically with SQA exams in mind. So, whether you are studying for Standard Grade, Intermediate, Higher or Advanced Higher, this book offers you an enormous range of ideas and strategies to make the study period for SQA exams that little bit more bearable, as well as explaining a little about how your exams are prepared and marked – information which might make the whole process a little bit clearer for you.

SQA has offices in both Glasgow and in Dalkeith (near Edinburgh) and employs over 750 people. Your school or college is one of over 1,470 centres authorised to deliver SQA courses. It is the national body responsible for the development, accreditation, assessment and certification of qualifications in Scotland (other than degrees). The qualifications are recognised around the world, and the SQA is known for quality, integrity and good service. So how does this affect you? Well, you are studying for exams that are fair and just, and I cannot think of a better organisation in terms of assistance to schools and to you.

In Scotland, SQA manages several different levels of courses leading to examinations and awards in a wide range of subjects. Before you read the next section, it's worth pointing out that SQA examination structures will be changing from 2013 onwards (and this book will be accordingly updated). But if you're preparing for exams before 2013, then here's what you should know...

For many students, Standard Grade courses ('S' Grades) are taken over two years (typically, in third and fourth years at secondary school, but also in many colleges). There are three levels of award:

◆ Foundation

◆ General

◆ Credit

The outcome is determined by the course content and an exam. These exams allow students to leave school, start training, go to college or progress further in school. Although the number of students taking Standard Grades has declined in recent years (see below), they still make up the largest number of exams taken each year in Scotland (over 358,000 entries in 2009). As part of the new future exam structures, it is worth pointing out that Standard Grade is due to be phased out (with the last exams in 2013) and replaced with new qualifications (called National 4 and National 5).

Some students will follow Access 2 or 3 courses in school. These courses have no exams and the outcome is determined by class work. In recent years, many schools have replaced teaching Standard Grades with National Courses lasting one year at Intermediate 1 and/or Intermediate 2. For students in fourth, fifth and sixth years at secondary school (as well as those at college), the four levels of award are:

1   Intermediate 1: generally for students who have a Foundation award at S Grade. There were over 65,000 Intermediate 1 entries in 2009.

2   Intermediate 2: usually for students who have (or would be likely to achieve) a General award at Standard Grade. This level can be 'stepping stone' to taking a Higher which normally follows on over the next two years. There were over 122,000 Intermediate 2 entries in 2009.

3   Higher: usually for students who have a credit award or an Intermediate 2 award. Higher courses are normally needed for entry to university or college to study for degrees, Higher National Certificates HNC) or Higher National Diplomas (HND). Highers are the most common examination awards for progress beyond school. There were over 167,000 Higher entries in 2009.

4   Advanced Higher: although relatively few students follow AH courses in sixth year (just under 20,000 entries in 2009), these awards are very useful for entry to university, college or the workplace.

The diagram below shows you how the SQA arranges all of these courses and how they all relate to each other.

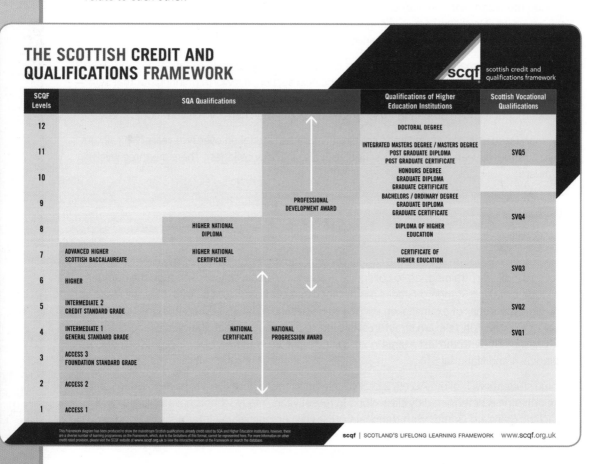

If nothing else, the information above should reassure you that you're not alone in having to prepare for your SQA exams…

Top Tip

SQA now offers past examination papers (going back at least three years) for these courses free of charge online, as well as marking instructions for each subject. These are available from SQA's website, www.sqa.org.uk. The quickest way to find them is to type 'past papers' into the Search box. You can also purchase printed sets of question papers and (sometimes condensed) answers from bookshops, online bookstores, or directly from the publishers Bright Red Publishing (www.brightredpublishing.co.uk).

It is worthwhile checking up on www.sqa.org.uk now. If you go to the homepage, you will see information for four groups. The section for you is the one named 'learners' (although there is nothing to stop you looking at the others sections as well). Here you will find the SQA timetable, and links to past papers, marking instructions, specimen question papers and comments from the markers allowing candidates to improve performance. There are several links and you can find out how to register for the results to be electronically delivered to you as well as links to UCAS (the organisation that manages applications to universities).

Of a more technical nature, there are links to the detailed course specifications, (written in a language more appropriate for teachers) and information regarding 'estimates' and what happens if you are absent on the day of the exam. The Scottish system has a unique 'appeal' system which works very much to your favour. SQA exams are fair, and generally 'you get what you deserve'. For more details of how exams are set and marked, their results are issued and so on, take a look at Chapter 4.

For the moment, I hope that this serves to reassure you about the organisation that sets SQA examinations. Now, let's have a look at the best way to approach those exams...

SO THEN, WHAT'S THIS STUDYING GAME ALL ABOUT?

To have reached this stage in your education I assume that you have, so far, done pretty well. You clearly have imagination, foresight and intelligence to have bought this book! After all, you could have spent the money on fast food, a DVD, the first eight minutes of a driving lesson, or even eleven minutes with a private tutor. You will certainly have experienced success before, whether it was in school, at home or in clubs, through hobbies, sport, leisure, music or whatever.

Question

SAQ 1 Spend a moment jotting down your successes in life. Take time to work out why you have had some success.

Answer

You may have achieved success through luck, charisma (my favourite!) or even bribery, but more likely through positive means, such as:

◆ being organised
◆ having a plan
◆ working hard and putting in the time

◆ practising the skills
◆ passion and enthusiasm
◆ support from others

Sometimes you can be held back, possibly by fear.

Question

SAQ 2 Write down your four main fears when it comes to studying for exams. If this book belongs to you, feel free to write in it! If it belongs to a library or to your school or college's supported study unit, then find a piece of paper instead…

As you go through this book, we shall have a look at the ways in which we can overcome many of these real fears.

I would imagine that you may have mentioned fears such as 'Am I clever enough to pass?, or, 'I don't know how to get organised and do my best', or, 'I go to pieces in an exam' or 'I can't remember all that stuff'. This book looks at all of those problems.

Possibly the best way to start, is to identify what you have to do in order to fail, so...

Question

?

SAQ 3   Make a list called 'How to fail an exam'.

Answer

I asked a bunch of Scotland's finest young people to do this for me and they came up with:

- don't revise ('revision is for wimps!')
- study and revise when you feel like it! (like 'tomorrow!')
- don't bother planning (who needs a schedule?)
- rely solely on the teacher to teach you everything
- write illegibly

- revise passively (if at all)
- 'tactics' to pass an exam – are they not little white mints?
- decide you can't be bothered... (there's something better on the telly!)
- turn up a day late for the exam

Answer continued ➢

Answer *continued*

- ◆ (this is genuine…) 'I'd rather go to a Killers gig'!
- ◆ miss all the deadlines
- ◆ panic with all my friends
- ◆ walk out of the exam early
- ◆ do all my work at the last moment
- ◆ mess up my timing during the exam
- ◆ think that you are going to fail
- ◆ don't bother reading the questions
- ◆ miss out part of the exam
- ◆ forget to come back in for Paper 2
- ◆ answer a question that was not asked for!

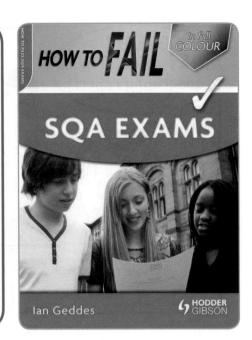

HOW TO **FAIL** ✓ SQA EXAMS

Ian Geddes

In full COLOUR

HODDER GIBSON

This list is just a sample. The point is that such a list is easy to produce, and in a sense I could end this book now and say to you: just do the opposite of the above! However, I suppose you want to get your money's worth…

Question

SAQ 4 Make a list of all the SQA courses you are studying this year. As with all SAQs in this book, if this is your own copy then write on the page below. If you're using the book as part of a school/college study skills class, you (or your teacher) can photocopy the grid.

For each course, assess your chances of success, your strengths and weaknesses. For each weakness try and identify a creative solution.

SQA Subject	SQA Level	Weakness	Strength and Solution	Target Grade

Many (many) years ago, I completed a course on 'the psychology of passing exams' (the things that you have to do to become a teacher!). The conclusion of ten fascinating hours of lectures was that exams only determine whether you can pass an exam, they don't necessarily prove that you know much about the subject. You know what? They gave us an exam to test us! I passed. The education system is still geared around exams, at least in your final years of formal school education.

Examinations are not just about memory. Research indicates that your ability to prepare for the exam and to be aware of what the system expects from you is of equal importance.

Reflection Time

Do you:

- set aside time regularly for homework and thinking about your work?
- usually spend time cramming the night before the exam?
- believe the more I study the less time I have for my friends and having fun?
- study with the TV on?
- spend three hours solid at studying, without a break?

When you look back at your notes:

- do they seem to be incomplete and messy?
- do you think: 'Where are my notes?'

Do you:

- re-read all your notes regularly?
- have problems remembering all the facts?
- fail to remember what you did yesterday, let alone last year?
- have no idea what will come up in the test or exam?
- think that if 'I only had time, my homework would be better'?
- think that you should have scored better or that your teacher is harsh/cruel/doesn't like you?

Do you:

- worry that your mind goes blank in a test?
- work best when the fear of failure kicks in?
- read slowly and worry that you can't get through all this work?
- ask how could you read faster?
- know what you want to say, but it never comes out that way on paper?

This book will address these issues. So come back to this page at the end of the book, and see how far you have come in terms of thinking, planning, revising and passing exams…

SOME BASICS

Tests! Exams! Assessments! Torture!

Question

SAQ 1 Why do we have exams?

Answer

Exams and tests are important for the following reasons:

◆ they measure your progress

◆ they encourage you to revise

◆ they are necessary to satisfy the conditions of the course

◆ they provide an 'entry level' for employment/college/university

Generally, society sets standards for moving on and recording progress. In Scotland, we have the SQA and they are responsible for setting, organising and certifying the courses that you are studying. Your teachers/tutors know exactly what skills and content are required, and you will be treated fairly.

What is the best way to prepare? Some people think that there are three stages to consider: the marathon, the 1500 metres and the 100 metres. Think of it like being an athlete.

Question

SAQ 2 So how would you prepare for a marathon, the 1500 metres and the 100 sprint?

Answer

The key features of preparing for a marathon (or long-term revision) e.g. for the exam at the end of the college/school year:

◆ have a plan

◆ be organised and keep notes secure

◆ review notes regularly

◆ write summary notes for the exam

◆ match notes to old tests/exam papers

◆ keep on top of folios/projects

◆ aim for understanding the notes rather than memorising them

◆ buy revision books or, better still, get your folks to buy them for you

◆ get anything you think you may need from your teacher/lecturer

◆ know what the system is

◆ check out revision/study websites

The key features of preparing for a 1500 metre middle distance race (a month or so before a test/exam):

◆ check how you are doing against the plan

◆ keep reading through the notes

◆ remember the importance of active revision

◆ practise answering old questions

◆ check the summary notes

◆ get friends over to talk through some of the tough stuff

◆ reinforce what you already know

◆ continue to check out revision/study websites

The key features of preparing for a 100 metre sprint (the last week or so before exams begin):

◆ check through past questions

◆ re-read the *How to Pass* books or other revision/study guides

◆ check through key cards or handouts

◆ concentrate on those parts that you have had difficulty with

◆ work with a friend and go over the basics

◆ check up on case study information if it applies to your course

◆ practise drawings/diagrams

◆ don't try anything new – all the learning should have been done by now!

◆ and, when you feel okay about it, stop, relax and get a decent sleep

HOW TO PASS SQA EXAMS

Revising

So what is good study?

A popular technique is the **SMART** approach to studying:

◆ **Specific:** make your targets quite clear and precise. Don't be vague. Don't say, 'I will study more'. Rather, say something like, 'I will plan a weekly timetable', or I will do my Maths homework tonight.

◆ **Measurable:** be able to measure your progress towards your goal, for example, after five weeks you will have passed a unit test or answered a question without a book on whatever you set as a target.

◆ **Action-related:** break down your study goals into a set of smaller tasks.

◆ **Realistic:** get real, otherwise you become disillusioned.

◆ **Time-based:** work out your tasks backwards from deadlines. Have a beginning and completion date for your goal.

Remember, your goals can have flexibility. If necessary, rewrite them (for example, if you were ill for a couple of weeks you would have to make changes to your targets). Sometimes we do not get things right first time. Plans are not rigid, you must be able to adapt and improve them. The last thing I want you to do is to abandon everything because you needed to take the cat to the vet!

Example

This is an example from a geography Higher, but the principles can be applied to any subject:

Specific: to be able to describe and explain the processes leading to selected 'glacial features'.

Measurable: to name eight basic glaciated erosion features (corrie, lochan, ribbon lake, u-shaped valley, truncated spur, arete, pyramidal peak, hanging valley).

Action-related: write two or three sentences about each feature, describe and explain them and draw the features.

Realistic: check your answer against old exam papers, try this under test conditions. Work at the descriptions and drawings that are not very good.

Time-based: Complete this by Thursday.

Question

SAQ 3 Create your own example. Select a couple of your subjects and attempt a SMART approach in the table below.

Specific	
Measurable	
Action-related	
Realistic	
Time-based	

Remembering

There are two main kinds of memory at work, whether you're at school, college or university: specific and general.

In areas such as science, mathematics, engineering and foreign languages, you mainly have to know the exact wording of formulae, rules, norms, laws, grammar or vocabulary. Regrettably, sometimes you just need to put in the hours it takes for reading, note-taking, drawing memory maps or any other technique that helps you to remember. Quite often in exams, complex formulae will be given. Surprisingly enough, this type of memory work ('specific memorising') is not as common as you may think. What is crucial is your ability to try and understand what it is you are remembering. This is also important in the second type of memory work, general memory work.

General memorising is important in all subjects. Here, it is important that you remember the general ideas and show a broad understanding of what it is you are studying. To assist you in all memory work, you should make use of note-taking techniques. Some people find that it is really useful to revise memory work with a friend. Others prefer to work alone.

Many years ago, I failed a physics exam at university. I know you find it difficult to believe, either because:

♦ I surely can't have failed anything, or

♦ You can't believe that I actually picked Physics as a subject.

Eventually I worked out what I was doing wrong. I was trying too hard to memorise the content. It was only when I devoted my time to trying to understand it that the content started to make sense. There is no point in trying to memorise the Periodic Table (in chemistry), without a grasp of the rationale of such a table, or trying to describe a moraine (geography) without a broad idea of what glaciers do.

Question

SAQ 4 Select a couple of your subjects, pick on a topic and try to jot down content that requires to be specifically memorised, and then generally memorised.

Mind you, I hit on another strategy with my daughter. I offered her £10 for each S Grade Credit pass and £25 for each Higher. I was delighted when it came time to pay up! Try negotiating similar deals with your folks! I was always intrigued that my daughters could remember the words of a thousand pop songs, but could not remember a single quote from Twelfth Night…

Reflection Time

Be honest. Think about how you go about revising and memorising at the moment. List four ways in which it could be improved.

Memory or concept mapping (mind maps)

Wikipedia defines a mind map as 'a diagram used to represent words, ideas, tasks, or other items linked to and arranged around a central key word or idea'. Mind maps are used to generate, visualise, structure and classify ideas. They are used as an aid in study, organisation, problem-solving, decision-making and writing. The elements that make up a mind map are arranged intuitively (naturally) according to the importance of the concepts they represent. These elements are grouped into branches or areas that they have in common. If you search for 'mind maps' online you will get over 82 million hits! So I guess it is a mainstream study technique. Tony Buzan is credited by many to be the guru of modern mind-mapping. Check out his website.

Mapping study topics is a technique that I used as a student years ago. It now seems to go under a variety of names, but I was first shown how to do it when I was studying geography. We called it mental mapping. My brain seldom works in neat lines. By working on key words, images and associations you can remember far more. Try it! Mental maps can be really useful for revision. I know a student who constructed a brilliant map of the book, *Catcher in the Rye*. It was so good she sold copies of it to her friends for £10 each. You see: this book not only helps you to pass SQA exams, but also gives you some business ideas!

This gave me an idea for a map: 'how to make money' . . .

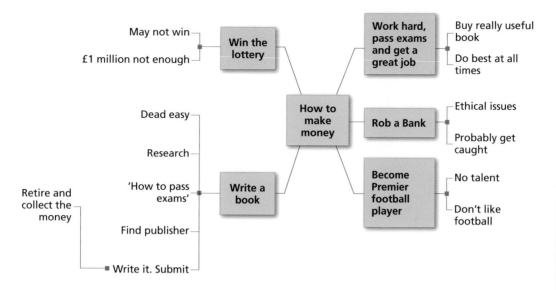

So what are the uses?

Mapping allows us to summarise information and consolidate data from a variety of sources. It can give us the big picture. A mental map never has to be complete. You can add to it at any time. It is personal to you, and you control the words and symbols. It is particularly helpful for visual learners (see the section later on). Mental maps are economic in terms of time. You do not need to write as much, and you can show trends and associations between ideas.

I asked one of my students about mental mapping. She said, 'I find it really useful. I use it to take notes in the class or when revising at home, and it's vital when I am planning essays. I find that my ideas flow more smoothly, and I'm able to think logically and work my way through a complex problem and arrive at a solution. I would also like to thank Mr Geddes for this brilliant advice: he was truly inspirational.' (Guess which bit I made up?)

Hints and Tips

- ◆ When you start to use mental maps, start with key words and keep it simple.
- ◆ Start from the centre of the page and work outwards, creating important themes (branches) and key sub themes (sub branches).
- ◆ Print words in block capitals rather than your handwriting.
- ◆ Use colour.
- ◆ Put ideas down as you think them up.
- ◆ If the map ends up lopsided then add paper. You are free to redraw the map only when you have run out of ideas.
- ◆ There are no rules, so be creative and have some fun. Mental maps belong to you.

I have drawn up a 'how to pass exams' map using this technique.

HOW TO PASS SQA EXAMS

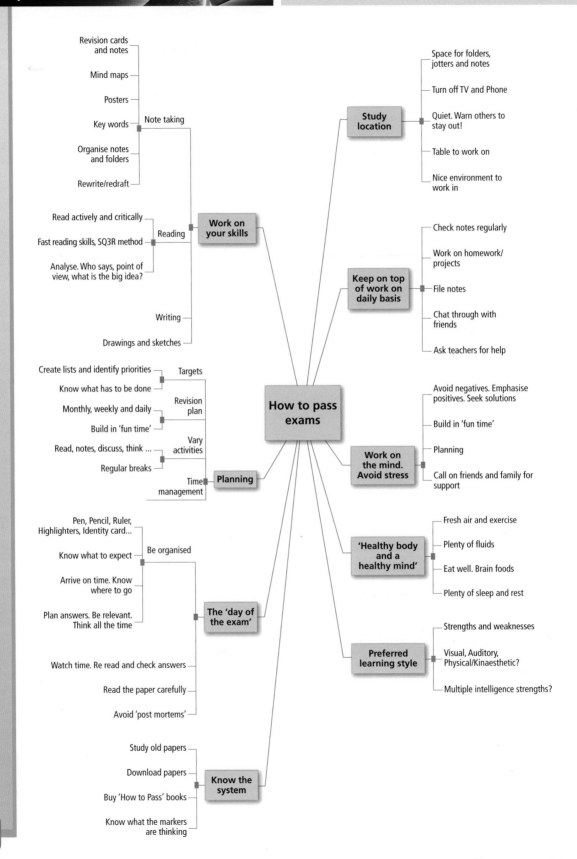

Revision cards and notes

Mind maps

Posters

Key words — Note taking

Organise notes and folders

Rewrite/redraft

Read actively and critically

Fast reading skills, SQ3R method — Reading — Work on your skills

Analyse. Who says, point of view, what is the big idea?

Writing

Drawings and sketches

Create lists and identify priorities — Targets

Know what has to be done

Monthly, weekly and daily — Revision plan

Build in 'fun time'

Read, notes, discuss, think ... — Vary activities

Regular breaks

Time management — Planning

Pen, Pencil, Ruler, Highlighters, Identity card...

Know what to expect — Be organised

Arrive on time. Know where to go

Plan answers. Be relevant. Think all the time

The 'day of the exam'

Watch time. Re read and check answers

Read the paper carefully

Avoid 'post mortems'

Study old papers

Download papers

Buy 'How to Pass' books — Know the system

Know what the markers are thinking

How to pass exams

Study location
- Space for folders, jotters and notes
- Turn off TV and Phone
- Quiet. Warn others to stay out!
- Table to work on
- Nice environment to work in

Keep on top of work on daily basis
- Check notes regularly
- Work on homework/ projects
- File notes
- Chat through with friends
- Ask teachers for help

Work on the mind. Avoid stress
- Avoid negatives. Emphasise positives. Seek solutions
- Build in 'fun time'
- Planning
- Call on friends and family for support

'Healthy body and a healthy mind'
- Fresh air and exercise
- Plenty of fluids
- Eat well. Brain foods
- Plenty of sleep and rest

Preferred learning style
- Strengths and weaknesses
- Visual, Auditory, Physical/Kinaesthetic?
- Multiple intelligence strengths?

Question

SAQ 5 In the table below, I have provided an outline of a map that could help you go through the process of buying a computer. Use the key words and complete your own map.

Central box	First link	Second link	Other links
Buying a computer	Laptop or PC?	how much do I have to spend?	savings job borrow steal (only joking!)
		specification research needed	memory screen size colour
		where to buy? advantages/ disadvantages	internet second hand electrical shop
		why do I need a computer?	homework access to internet social networks

SAQ 6 Create your own map. Select a fairly small theme to start with. After a few tries you will quickly get the hang of it. It's a great technique.

How to read, write and take notes

For many people these skills are the key ingredients of studying and passing exams. These skills are linked.

Reading

This is one of the key skills. We read for fun and for gathering information and it is one of the key skills required in education and for life.

How many times have you read a few pages in a book and then realised that you have taken in absolutely nothing? In fact how many times have you read these lines?

The first thing to consider is what the **purpose** of your reading is, and to read accordingly. So are you trying to:

◆ find out more about a topic?

◆ help you remember 'facts'?

◆ collect information to complete homework or a project?

◆ get a broad understanding of a theme?

◆ get in depth knowledge and understanding?

◆ help you pass an exam?

Whatever you decide to read, the chances are that you'll need to get a grip of the 'big' or main idea. This can be for a whole book, a chapter or maybe just a paragraph.

Following on from knowing the purpose of your reading is **extracting the important details**. Again, this will be linked to the 'big' idea. Check out the SQ3R method...

What You Should Know

SQ3R is really useful for complex and detailed reading.
It is what we call a 'staged' approach. This method seems to be a successful way to sharpen your study skills. SQ3R stands for:

Step 1 Survey/Scan
Get an overall picture of what you're going to study *before* you study it. Read the first and last paragraphs. Notice headings, pictures, images, graphs and diagrams. Flick backwards and forwards through the pages. This should all be done quickly.

Step 2 Question
Ask questions such as 'what, why, how, when, who and where?' What do you already know about this topic? What do you need to find out?

Step 3 Read
Read actively. You can 'speed read'. Read in a relaxed yet focused way. Don't agonise over difficult ideas or words. Do not stop to look up difficult words. Do not take notes.

Step 4 Recall/Remember
Turn the book over. Recall headings, important ideas and connect things you have just read. Test your memory. Jot down some points without looking back at the text. Go back to the text and check that you have got the key points

Step 5 Review
Survey what you have just covered. It may involve some notes or simply thinking. Imagine how you might explain what you've read to someone else. Some people may wish to read a second time.

How many times have you read a few pages in a book and then realised that you have taken in nothing? Experts tell us that we can concentrate for no longer than 40 minutes without a break. (Is that why most lessons last 50 to 60 minutes?) So read with a purpose. Eliminate distractions. Remember to add to your reading an active task, such as some notes or highlighting.

Be aware of the exact purpose of your reading. On holiday, I can be found reading thrillers, golf magazines and even the latest 'Broons' or 'Oor Willie' book. I read for fun, to be entertained and for knowledge. You selected your subjects so remember there is nothing to stop you from being interested in what you read. The more you read, the more you will get into the subject and, usually, the more interesting it will become.

So what do we mean by 'active reading?'

This book encourages 'active' participation, by including SAQs and Reflection Time. Not all books will do this. But you can still stop regularly and do something 'active'. This includes making bullet point notes or speaking out loud to yourself about what you have learnt (always likely to get your mum to come to the door and check that you're okay!) or even highlighting the key sections with a marker.

Stop now and reflect on what you have learnt in this Chapter so far.

Activities

So how fast do you read?

I read recently that a 'speed reader' managed to complete one of the Harry Potter 600+ page books in a couple of hours. Is it possible? What can you take in and what can you remember? The evidence seems to support the view that a person who practises this skill can read at over 250 words a minute and can remember well. The two key issues are:

◆ use of peripheral vision

◆ the ability to absorb clusters of words rather than single words

Try reading this...

A   new   wave-power   machine   that   could   generate   up   to   ten   times   more   energy   than   existing   versions   may   turn   out   to   be   our   saviour.

Obviously you were concentrating and reading single words. Now try this…

A new wave-power machine   that could generate   up to ten times more energy than existing versions   may turn out to be our saviour.

With some practise you can read in small chunks like this far faster, and the research indicates that reading slowly can actually inhibit learning!

Question

SAQ 7   Make a list of your reading over the last week, or keep a diary of your reading for the next week. What have you read? Why?

SAQ 8   Select an article from a paper, magazine or from a course, and identify the 'big' idea and some important detail.

More and more students use online material. That is fine but here is a cautionary word of warning: you could find yourself reading material in the form of 'blogs', 'wikis' and other websites where the information is presented in a different way to textbooks, and you might have to search a little harder for evidence that stands up to critical scrutiny. Be careful. Do not unquestioningly accept that what you read is accurate. It can be wrong, biased or just mischievous.

Hard words and tricky sentences

You will come across unfamiliar words and difficult sentences. Don't panic if you do not understand everything. There are a few strategies you can adopt.

◆ **Use a dictionary**. You may have one at home, or you can borrow one from the school or college. You can also use an online dictionary that comes free with many word-processing packages. SQA exams do not use obscure words or jargon in their questions.

◆ **Look for clues**. Often there are clues in the rest of the text. The general context of the sentence or paragraph will provide you with some clues. Look ahead, and see where the argument goes.

◆ **Take a note** of the section/word, and ask your teacher or tutor about it later.

◆ **Ask yourself if it really matters**.

Reflection Time

Think back over this Chapter so far and reflect on what you may change in your reading habits as a result of these few pages.

Writing

This is another of the key skills in education. Once again when you are preparing for and sitting examinations then you will be required to write.

Question

SAQ 9   Make a list of your writing over the last week, or keep a diary of your writing for the next week. What have you written? Why?

Answer

◆ we scribble lists or jot down bullet points

◆ we write to help us remember

◆ we write to pass information to our friends/tutors/teachers

◆ we write to show someone or even ourselves that we understand

◆ we might re-write notes to assist remembering and understanding

◆ we write to help convince somebody that we should pass an exam

Can you think of any other reason?

Writing shows that you can meet the expectations of the marking criteria. It demonstrates your intellectual ability to others. It also shows your ability to analyse and explain complex ideas.

Sometimes you write notes you'll want to keep. Some notes will be thrown away. As I write this book, I am discarding notes written to assist me in the structure of this chapter.

I am trying to think of any exam that does not involve some writing. At the moment I cannot think of any. Perhaps a practical music exam?

Question

SAQ 10 Work with a friend and make a list of the key steps in writing an effective exam essay. Take alternative turns.

Answer

read the general instructions
read through all the questions
check the marks and budget time accordingly
select the questions to be answered
underline the key words in the question
only now are you ready to write anything!
plan your answer
write your answer referring to your plan
remember a beginning, middle and an end
proofread it
final check: have you answered all the parts? Move on.

Summary

A good essay is:

Well focused: it answers all parts of the question. Stick to the actual question. Avoid waffle.

Well organised: planned and structured. Tell the marker what you are going to do, do it and then tell her/him what you have done.

Well supported: will have facts, evidence, examples, quotes, named sources, case study details and/or dates.

Well packaged: is legible handwriting important? Yes. Is spelling important? Yes

Is grammar important? Yes. Remember that you need to communicate your ideas under the stress of exam conditions.

So do your best and always try to leave time to proofread. Markers can deduct marks for badly written work and you penalise yourself if they cannot read your work. Often marks refer to a principal marker before taking this decision. Practise handwriting to develop your own style.

Taking notes

This is a skill that must be learnt and practised. It is so easy to overdo the note-taking. Valuable time is spent on the physical chore of writing notes with little effort on knowing what it is you are writing about. If you are going through a 'bumper' pack of 500 A4 sheets every few days then you are overdoing it! The trouble is that there is a 'feel good' factor in note taking. You have something as physical evidence that shows that you have been working. But have you been making best use of your time?

Depending on the task, you may need to manipulate information from several sources, such as textbooks, articles, reviews or websites. Some sources will be 'dip in and out', while some will require more intensive reading. You need to decide the purpose for note-taking.

Why bother taking notes?

◆ Are they to help you express ideas about the course in your own words?

◆ Are they intended to summarise a range of course materials?

◆ Are they to help you remember what you did today in a class?

◆ Are they for a particular essay or project?

◆ Are they simply to assist you in active reading?

◆ To help you think through course ideas?

◆ To keep a record of examples, useful points, quotes?

◆ To aid memory?

◆ To prepare for an assignment?

◆ Will they provide an overview of the subject?

◆ Will the notes create a summary of different viewpoints?

Hints and Tips

Always write your notes in your own words. If you just copy, then the chances are that you will not understand as well.

Beware of plagiarism. This is when you copy someone else's work, don't acknowledge it, and then pass it off as your own. This is not acceptable, and will be penalised very heavily (usually with a 'no award' result). If you are writing a critical comment on a piece of literature, be very careful that you never plagiarise. If you are taking notes from a book, jot down which book and page. Of course you can use direct quotations, but always note where you got it from.

Techniques for taking notes

You need to sort out a **filing system**. Perhaps invest in some ring binders, dividers and plastic pockets. Whatever you do, you must spend time keeping your notes logical and legible. Date your work, number pages, link the notes with source books, handouts or jotters.

Remember that '**less is more**'. Don't crowd a page or card, Work on reducing the material down to individual A4 sheets or cards. Try using index cards. Just the perfect size and easy to carry around.

Make the notes **visual**. Use sketches, diagrams, mind maps. Use colour. You work out what suits you the best. Decide whether to number the points. Or use 'bullet points'. However, you have to go beyond simply copying or colouring endless paragraphs with a highlighter pen and kidding yourself that you are learning...

Increasingly, students like to put their notes in **computer files**. A portable storage device such as a pen drive (flash disk or memory stick) can be very useful. But make sure that you back it up! I find that Powerpoint is good for note taking. The trouble is that you may be slow at typing and you focus trying to create a perfect set of notes. Time can be wasted getting to that point of perfection.

There are good **websites** that already have well worked sets of notes. These are good, but remember if you produce your own notes then the chances are you will understand them far better. However, it is a trade off between time and usefulness and you must decide what is best for you.

Of course you cannot write on your school or college textbooks. But you can make notes on your **own books** and on **handouts**. I appreciate that we are taught from an early age not to do this. However, when it is your book, you are free to do so. The chances are that you will not be selling the book on eBay!

Some students find that taking **audio notes** is best for them. Try talking into your computer, mobile or ipod to help you explain things in your own words.

I really encourage the use of **summary cards**. I find the cards 20 cms by 12 cms are ideal (around A5 size). That size is big enough to jot down notes and sketches, but small enough to fit in a book or pocket. Many students find that, as the exam approaches, it is possible to re work the notes, and as you do this then a whole section of a unit can be reduced down to a single card.

Finally, make sure your notes are personalised. They will make more sense to you. Date them.

Question

SAQ 11 Start with a newspaper article. Take some notes. Practise this regularly. Avoid copying long sections. You learn more by putting the article into your own words. It forces you to think far more.

Time management

'You can never add minutes to a day. You can only make more use of those minutes wisely'. A great philosopher came up with that quote. (Me!)

Mind you, you could always add an hour to the day by getting up earlier! Sorry, only joking. A popular chocolate bar used to advertise the importance of 'a Mars a day helps you work, rest and play'. So get the balance of your time right.

Question

SAQ 12 Score yourself on the following time management questionnaire: 2 points for 'always', 1 point for 'sometimes' and 0 for 'never'. Be honest!

I do things in order of priority.

I get done what needs to be done that day.

I get my work in on time.

I know I use my time effectively.

I make time to plan what I have to do.

If I have a tough task, I get stuck in.

I make up daily/ weekly 'to do' lists.

I can prioritise things I must do first.

I meet deadlines without rushing.

I hit my project/homework deadlines on time.

I hate hanging about waiting.

I am usually early for meetings.

I am up to date in my reading.

I make sure I am not interrupted when on task.

I cut out the trivia.

I think I spend enough time on my course work.

I do the most important tasks when I am sharpest.

I regularly check my targets.

I know what I have to do today.

I am happy with the way I use my time.

Answer

34–40 points	Congratulations. Not so sure why you need this book!
28–33 points	You are generally a good time manager. Still a little yet to learn.
22–27 points	You are managing your time fairly well.
16–21 points	You are giving yourself extra stress. Think hard about time management. This book is a great investment!
16–0 points	Some may say that your planning and use of time is out of control.

There are 168 hours in a week. Take off nine hours a day for sleeping and eating. So what is reasonable for study? It depends, of course. There are more demanding months than others. Even if you set aside 15 hours a week, for studying then you can divide it into segments and use it strategically. Time to read, take notes, work on projects. Take time to divide all tasks into smaller sub tasks. Set targets for each session. The more you define your work into small, discrete concrete tasks, the more control you have over it. Most computers have programmes built in with daily planners and 'to do' lists which can help you.

Question

SAQ 13 The first step is to prioritise tasks. Look at the grid below. It was based on the idea of an American, Steven Covey.

Make a list of ten or more things that you have to do. Include school work or anything you have to do in your leisure time or time in the house. Place those items in the best box in this grid. There are four variable elements. For example if, 'keeping your room free from rats' is not important and not urgent, place this task in Box 4.

Important Urgent	Not important Urgent
      Box 1	 Box 2
Important Not urgent	Not important Not urgent
      Box 3	 Box 4

When it comes to action you should first focus on the tasks which are both urgent and important, i.e. Box 1. So work your way through the boxes in order, 1 to 4. Sometimes, I jump to a Box 4 task. Usually these tasks will be quickly completed and you get an immediate feeling of progress. You feel good and can then move on to a more demanding task in Box 2 or Box 1.

A problem that some students have is 'perfectionism', the need to have everything spot on. This can result in a feeling of failure even when what has been managed is good. This takes us back to **realistic targets**.

Another issue is **procrastination** (if you've read Hamlet, you'll know all about that). Procrastination is putting off getting started. The fear of failure is sometimes enough. Don't put off your work to wait for the perfect opportunity. It will never come!

25

Question

SAQ 14 What must you do every day? Make a list of what time is already committed and allocate a certain number of hours to it.

You may well have included sleeping, washing, eating, going to school, chores in the house, attending a music lesson…

What we are left with is time that you can still allocate to study. Some days have more 'allocated' time, others have less. It changes at the weekend and during holidays. I would advise you to plan your time on a weekly basis.

Question

SAQ 15 So, apart from your allocated times, what else would you like to do in a week?

As the exams approach, you will have to reallocate the balance between 'fun' time and revision. How much study time can you fit in? Be realistic. Four hours every night is crippling, but 15 hours spread over a week should be about right. You can decide when to timetable those study hours.

Question

SAQ 16 Time to build up your own draft 'planning timetable'. In the Appendices you will find a simple grid template for a weekly study planner. Use this as a starting point. In time, you may well design a better version which better fits your needs, or find one on the internet or on a computer scheduler.

I carry a diary, and I have also created one on my work computer with a daily 'to do' list. I also have a forward planner which lists things coming up over the next month or so. I try not to get caught out with the 'expected unexpected!'

With the 'to do' list, jot down things that must, should or will later need to be done. This list varies in length from day to day. Some people believe that this is a better way of prioritising than the Covey Grid. I have great satisfaction ticking off each success. It is important to create a priority ranking within the list.

A something that **must** be done without delay

B something that **should** be done as soon as possible

C something that **can be left for the moment**, but may become a B or A, if left too long

However, should you attend to a few early 'C's and feel good, or apply yourself to a difficult 'A'? The answer is, 'something that must be done without delay', should always be top priority.

Question

SAQ 17 Design your own 'to do' form. A suggestion is provided below.

To do	A, B or C	Date completed
1		
2		
3		
4		
5		
6		
7		

Hints and Tips

- Pareto's principle (the 80–20 rule). This states that 80 per cent of the result can usually be gained by concentrating on the most important 20 per cent of the task!
- Regularly check your study calendar and be aware of approaching deadlines.
- Mark or highlight parts of your reading which are holding you up. Skip past them. Go back later.
- Keep on top of your notes.
- Don't waste time. If you mess about in school, you lose out. That time or opportunity may never be found again.

Question

SAQ 18 Look at these three case studies. What would you suggest that could be done? Give each student three pieces of advice.

Susan often delays starting an assignment because she is worried about her writing ability, which leads to a fear of getting started. She rarely leaves enough time to redraft and proofread work so her writing is full of unnecessary errors. Susan is afraid of failing, but her fear is leading to the thing that worries her most.

John keeps missing deadlines for handing in assignments and projects. He often underestimates the length of time it takes to complete the

Questions continued ➤

Question continued

different stages of writing essays and completing the reports. Although he is very able and competent, the end grade is lower because things appear to be rushed.

Amelia thinks that she studies best when the pressure is on. It hasn't let her down yet. However there is so much to do and so little time to do it in, there seems to be no point in doing anything because it won't be enough! She sings in a band and some weeks there is no time to study.

Remember

Get organised: it has been calculated that the typical senior school/college student wastes three weeks a year searching for misplaced information.

Create a plan: identify your priorities.

Create a tidy and organised working area: this makes you feel good. Concentrate on one task at a time. Finish what you start, but don't ever start more than you can finish in a session!

Reflection Time

Think of three things that you can do today that could improve your chances of getting the basics right with studying in the future.

Homework

Question

SAQ 19   Briefly write down how you handle your homework. Do you keep a diary of what is due and when or do you trust it all to memory?

SAQ 20   Think of some reasons why teachers give you homework.

Personally, I like to spoil your fun, keep you inside when you would rather be out with your friends, and of course it's what your parents expect! I know how most of you work. You get a week to do your homework, and that means you start it on the way to school or college on the bus. Bad idea! If you do it this way, the job will be rushed and it will show.

Homework should allow you to keep up to date and act as a check to find out how you are doing and when well done, it gives you a good feeling. Quality work is useful for revision. Homework allows you to investigate subjects more fully than time allows in school. Homework allows you to develop good study attitudes, in particular, a sense of self discipline. This is vital when you go on to college or university. It also allows you to be responsible for your learning and to manage time and meet deadlines. So there!

The trouble is that sometimes teachers/tutors can be unfair. 'Just finish that off at home for tomorrow'! Sometimes they have no idea that you are studying other subjects and that you cannot do everything to the standard that you would want. Sometimes the work is never marked. If you are struggling, you can mention this to your teacher/tutor and see if you can negotiate a solution. Most teachers or tutors are extremely fair people.

Often the work is linked to exam style questions. Take care with it. You arrive home and your mum asks you if you have homework. The answer is usually, 'no' but that's not really true. Remember, homework can simply involve reading and organising the work you have done that day, and getting organised for the next day. Most schools or colleges have quiet places available at lunchtime for you to go and work. Schools often have homework clubs or 'supported study' times. Make the most of these. For those of you in your final year at school, you may have what you call 'free periods'. Now, this is the time that schools like to call 'study time'. So how do you spend it? A common room is usually not the place for productive work…

I can appreciate that after a long day at school you may not feel that you can immediately get stuck into your work the moment you come in the front door. You deserve a break. Also, some students might think it makes them look like a swot! So what strategies are you going to use to overcome that?

Question

SAQ 21 Write down the advantages of leaving your homework until the last possible moment. Did you think of any? I couldn't.

For Practice

Pause for reflection and review.

Learning habits

	Usually	Sometimes	Rarely
Do you study regularly?			
Do you work for short periods and take breaks?			
Do you plan your study and revision?			
Do you file away all your notes?			
Do you keep them labelled, making sure they are complete?			

For Practice continued ➤

For Practice *continued*

Dealing with information

	Usually	Sometimes	Rarely
Do you make simple diagrams to help you remember things?			
Do you regularly take notes and read through these notes?			
Do you add information to your notes as you go along?			
Do you draw up 'mental maps?'			

Understanding

	Usually	Sometimes	Rarely
If you struggle to understand, do you keep at it until you do?			
Do you ask your teacher if you fail to understand an idea?			
Do you actively question your understanding of what you read and see?			

If you have answered 'usually' to all ten of the questions, then you have little need for this book! Donate it to Oxfam! If not, keep going.

Finding the right space to study

◆ Can I use it whenever I need to?

◆ Is it free from both interruptions and distractions? If not give some thought as to how best to control your study environment.

◆ Does it have enough space for all my notes and study materials? Ideally you need a desk to write and read at and a comfortable (but not too comfortable) chair. Squatting down on the floor or on a bed is possibly not the most suitable place.

◆ What about the temperature and the available light? You may have to negotiate with a brother or sister if you share a room with them, and seek help and support from your parents.

Make the space your space. Keep it calm and peaceful. Avoid noisy areas with major distractions. Keep a waste paper bin handy. Have a fixed place for everything. Try to tidy up as you go along, by making the bed, hanging away clothes, getting rid of the dirty plates… half eaten kebabs should not be filed in the sock cupboard with your chemistry notes!

Habits

Do not study immediately after a meal and stop studying half an hour before bed. Have your plan and priorities thought out. Study in chunks of time no more than 45 minutes or so. Take breaks. Reward yourself when you have completed a task. To avoid boredom, change topics regularly.

Do you know when your energy level is at its highest? I could not study after ten pm. My levels were highest in the morning, and the early evening. That is when I tackled the more difficult parts of the course. When your levels are low, work on the easier and more enjoyable bits. Doing this will pay dividends almost immediately.

In the classroom

Try to sit near the front. Avoid distractions. This is where the learning often starts. Make sure you ask for assistance. Wait behind if need be for that extra help. Make sure that you go home with all your notes and everything that could be of use. Don't allow students less interested in passing their exams to put you off!

At home

It is easy to get 'past papers'. You can download them free of charge or buy printed versions (see page 5). They illustrate the types of questions that have come up in the last few years and the structure of the paper.

There are also some really good revision books aimed at Scottish students preparing for SQA exams, from three main publishers: Leckie and Leckie, Bright Red Publishing and Hodder Gibson, who publish this book and many others in the award-winning and SQA-endorsed

How to Pass range, as well as their Scottish Examination Materials series and a large range of classroom textbooks.

Put up a sign to avoid being disturbed. Make yourself unavailable for phone/mobile calls, emails etc. Give Facebook a break for a couple of hours. Leave these distractions in another room!

Planning

◆ Create an overview of what you want to revise. Reduce the work into manageable chunks.

◆ Use a weekly/monthly planner.

◆ Make sure that you have past papers. Use them!

◆ Set goals for each session.

◆ Have a break for ten minutes in every hour. Get up and move about!

◆ Use active revision rather than passive activity.

◆ Reward yourself when things have gone well.

◆ Practise writing out detailed answers (under timed/exam conditions) and draft outline answers.

'To do' list and a daily/weekly planner

I am a diary writer, and I have been since I was in first year in secondary school. My old diaries are treasured possessions. Whilst this style of diary is useful for recording your life, you need to have a diary that is going to help you plan. Your school/college may have given you a diary or planner. Use it! Go online and you will see lots of individual designs. Find something that suits you. Some people use a mental/mind map to help plan out homework and revision week by week.

Get organised!

Most students see the value of using folders and ring binders. However, there is a problem. Often more time and creative skill is used in colouring the covers than keeping the notes organised. So, what are the rules? Is it best to carry just one folder to school/college with all the active work? (Otherwise you could end up damaging your back carrying an overloaded bag. It is embarrassing pushing a Tesco trolley into school with all 11 binders!)

With one folder or binder you can take out the work completed every day or so and file at home in the individual subject folders. Label your folders. Invest in a hole puncher and dividers. When you file the notes, date all the pages and, if necessary, number all the pages. This will save you having to sort out the notes again if you accidentally drop the binder and the notes fly off in every direction.

If you are absent, find out what you have missed and take time to catch up and get the notes.

Get your social life sorted out

Continue to have a life! Meet up with your friends, play music, see films, whatever else you like to do.

The only difference is that you need to have the amount of time available for this planned out and you can't overdo it. You can party when the exams are over and really party when the results come in.

So remember...

Believe in yourself. You have a whole range of skills and you would not actually be on the course if you had not shown ability in the past! Be realistic! Success is great, but keep things balanced. Set yourself challenging but achievable goals.

What else can you do?

So what about revision books and past papers? Unfortunately, the act of buying a book, does not guarantee success. You need to be on top of your notes and follow advice given by your teachers/tutors too.

Once a section of any course has been taught, the best thing you can do, once you have sorted out your notes, is to work through the past papers, either from published copies or the free online ones on the SQA website.

Resist the temptation to go straight to the answers or the more detailed marker instructions on the website. You need to think, reflect and work at your answers. Then check it against the answers suggested. Remember that the suggested answers tend to be summarised and you will also come up with alternative relevant points that will always be accepted – refer to the marker instructions for more detail than the suggested answers will give you. Practise writing out answers in timed conditions.

Get to know the syllabus and the structure of the paper. work out timings so that you know how long you will have to tackle each question. Keep track of which 'options' you are studying and practise your answers to the right parts of the papers. On the SQA website it is possible to download the 'arrangement documents' for all your subjects. Be aware they will probably seem boring and detailed: they are written for the teacher/tutor. But these documents will be a useful reference as they give you the precise content of the course and of the exam.
On the SQA website you will find a section called 'services for learners'. There is a link to 'study skills and strategies'. Check it out.

Although I am a geographer, I have tried to ensure that this book is relevant for any SQA examination, and have asked my colleagues from a variety of subjects what particular skills and tips they could give to you. Nearly all the points mentioned are covered in this book. However, it is worth emphasising a few particular ones:

◆ In some subjects with an emphasis on **essay writing or extended writing** (e.g. history or English) you need to be very careful in establishing the exact task. If 10, 20 or even 30 marks are at stake, then a failure to interpret the question could be enough to result in a fail. In such questions it is so important to get the timing right.

◆ In modern languages, and most other subjects, it is important to draw on your knowledge acquired over many weeks and months, and **adapt** that **to fit the particular question** asked. It is vital that you are familiar with your dictionary and don't cut back on the time you spend on vocabulary revision. In French or German, verb tenses are so important.

Tips for multiple choice questions

◆ Read the question carefully and think of what your answer would be before you look at the choices available. Read the choices to see if your answer is there. If so, it is probably right, but read the other answers quickly to be certain.

◆ If the answer you were hoping for is not there, then read all the choices carefully and start to eliminate some that you know are wrong – cross these out. When you have narrowed your choices to two, try out each option with the question to see if they both definitely make sense.

◆ If you are confused by questions which offer 'all of the above' and 'none of the above' as possible answers then leave them blank and go back to them later. Put a mark beside any questions that you leave blank so that you'll know to come back to them – and leave yourself enough time to do this!

◆ If you aren't sure what a particular word means, look for clues. Think about the meanings of the prefix (beginning bit of a word) or suffix (end bit of a word). You could compare it to other words that start with the same letters. For example, the prefix 'epi' is found in the word epidermis, which refers to the top layer of the skin. What information can you take from that and then apply to a question about a plant called an 'epiphyte'? Would it have roots that stretch deep into the dirt or would it grow on the surface of something? More often than not your gut reaction will be the correct choice.

◆ If all else fails guess! Research shows that you should choose the 'B' or 'C' options!

(adapted from www.about.com)

Which answer should you choose for a multiple choice question?

A The one you didn't choose last time, they'd never have two in a row with the same choice as the right answer.

B None of them, leave it blank in case you look stupid for getting it wrong.

C The one that makes the prettiest pattern in the column of answers.

D None of the above.

Chapter 3

USE YOUR BRAIN!

When I was a boy, it was claimed that we only used 40 per cent of our brain. When I started teaching it had been changed to 30 per cent. Now we know that we are consciously using less than one per cent of our brain. Mind you, I've known some pupils over the years who can beat that (try 0.01 per cent!).

As a teacher, I have always known that students react in different ways to the activities in the class. Some like to work in a group whilst others prefer to be alone. I want to introduce some ideas about:

◆ the structure of the brain
◆ learning styles
◆ multiple and emotional intelligence
◆ differences in learning linked to gender

The structure of the brain

Scientists have explored theories about the two halves (hemispheres) of the brain, and the ways in which they differ in function and control of our body. Your dominant brain type has a significant effect on your study and exam revision pattern. It seems that your personality is significantly shaped by your brain type.

Right and left brain dominant characteristics

Left hemisphere style (verbal)	Right hemisphere style (visual)
responds to verbal instructions	responds to demonstrated instructions
logical problem solver	solves problem with hunches
good at spotting differences	looks for patterns and similarities
planned and structured	fluid and spontaneous
prefers talking and writing	prefers drawing
likes multiple choice tests	likes uncertain information
controls feelings	prefers open ended questions
likes hard facts	intuitive
prefers quiet study/ bright lights	impulsive
rational and analytical	likes to move around
likes order and tidy notes/ jotters	likes to study with music
objective	risk taker

Question

SAQ 1 Have a look at the list and work out which side you tend to favour. Put a tick beside each description that really matches your approach. Add up the ticks, and see where your strengths lie.

Left hemisphere score: Right hemisphere score:

So are you a left or right hemisphere learner?

It is possible to be a balanced right/left learner?

Whilst you go with your strengths, it is important to work a little at your weaknesses. After all, to pass exams you will need a wide range of skills.

From the list above you can work out that left hemisphere thinkers are keen to analyse, seek order and keep structured notes. You like to break down tasks into little bites and you try to logically revise all notes in an orderly way. Your room will probably be tidy, and you will have a plan up on the wall!

Question

SAQ 2 Sort out the following characteristics into 'left' and 'right' brain students.

◆ you take notes but often lose them
◆ you work with a 'to do' list
◆ you take time to make up your mind
◆ you are a critic
◆ you are good with people
◆ you're good at maths and science
◆ you may seem 'dreamy' but you're really deep in thought
◆ you're rational are logical
◆ people may have told you that you are sensitive
◆ your research is precise
◆ you think there are two sides to a story
◆ you set goals for yourself
◆ you often lose track of time
◆ you aren't 'touchy feely'
◆ you are spontaneous
◆ you can listen to a long lecture
◆ you're fun and witty
◆ you like action movies

Question continued ➢

Question *continued*

- ◆ you get lost!
- ◆ you read sitting up
- ◆ you read lying down
- ◆ you don't let feelings get in the way

Have you cracked the logic? The odd lines are 'right brain' characteristics, the even lines are for 'left brain' types.

Reflection Time

Think about how you can adapt your learning to compensate for your weaker brain side.

From the list above, if you are a right hemisphere learner, you will be creative and individualistic in your approach to study. You may well search out information on random searches online, and keep in touch with your friends. Planning is not your 'forte' and you resist attempts by your parents and teachers to minutely plan everything. You will be creative in your research with mind maps, sketches and use of 'highlighter' pens.

Current research indicates that you should go with your strengths but be aware of your weaknesses and attempt to introduce new/alternative hemisphere approaches at any opportunity. If you say 'I can't do that', then you could be heading for a self-fulfilling prophecy on failure.

Of course, some people think this is all a bit of a laugh and as realistic as the 'Easter Bunny' whilst others set great store by such approaches. As always, it's up to you to decide what suits you best.

Learning styles

So how do you think and train your mind? There are three main recognised systems of learning. So what sort of learner are you? Daft question! What does that mean? A learning style is a way of how you take in information. It is important to work out what style suits you. Check out the three possible styles below: **visual**, **auditory** and **physical/kinaesthetic**.

Activity	Visual	Auditory	Physical/Kinaesthetic
Spelling	Do you try to see the word? Do you see images?	Do you sound out the word?	Do you need to write down the word to see if it feels right?
Talking	Do you 'switch off' when people start to talk for too long?	Do you want to listen and talk?	Do you like to use your hands and gesture when you talk?
Concentrating	Are you distracted by movement or mess?	Are you distracted by sound and noise?	Are you distracted by hustle and bustle around you?
Meeting someone known to you	Do you remember faces but forget names?	Do you remember names and things you talked about but forget faces?	You may remember the names but you certainly remember what you did
Contacting people not known to you	Do you prefer 'face to face' meetings?	Do you prefer to use the telephone? Text? Email?	Do you like to talk but you prefer to walk or have a coffee with them?
Reading	Do you prefer description, allowing you to visualise?	Do you enjoy dialogue and like to 'hear' the characters talk?	Do you prefer 'action' stories? Or possibly you are not so keen on reading.
Examples of what you may say	'I see what you mean'	'That sounds good to me'	'I'm getting to grips with this now'

Adapted from Accelerated Learning, *Colin Rose (1987)*

Some bright person summed up these three styles as the **VAK** approach (get it?).

Are you a visual learner?

Such learners work best when information is presented in a written, diagrammatic or graphic form or language. Do you do best when you have handouts and notes? Do you take detailed written notes from textbooks? If yes, then you are probably a visual learner. Mind maps help you to generate ideas and make associations. I find them really useful as a memory aid. See the separate section on mind mapping on page 14. I know of students who decorate their room with brightly coloured 'post it' notes. This works well for them.

A visual learner:

◆ is good at spelling but forgets names

◆ needs quiet study time

◆ likes colours and fashion

◆ dreams in colours

Are you an auditory learner?

Do you prefer to learn by listening to the teacher and discussing issues in class? Do you find yourself reading aloud or talking things out to gain understanding? Do you like to talk through your work with your friends? If yes, then you are probably an auditory learner.

An auditory learner:

◆ is not afraid to speak out in class

◆ is good at explaining

◆ remembers names

◆ enjoys music

◆ reads slowly

Are you a physical/kinaesthetic learner?

Such people learn from a 'hands on' approach, and you may prefer to make things and learn, working in a lab or through being creative. If this approach suits you, then you are a physical/ kinaesthetic learner (sometimes also referred to as a 'tactile' learner).

Such a learner:

◆ is good at sports

◆ can't sit still for long

◆ is not great at spelling

◆ studies with loud music on

◆ is fidgety

Reflection Time

It is likely that you are studying anything between four and eight courses at school, and a variety of methods will be used. If you study, for example, a language, history and art, then you will need to use all three styles. However, you should always learn through your strengths and work on the weaknesses. Think about what you can now do to widen out your own learning style.

Remember that the brain is complex. A lot is packed into a tight space! If you appreciate how it works, then you can have more control over how you work, think and study.

Gender issues

The pass rates for subjects vary according to gender. Why? This is a really complex area and examination boards, schools and all sorts of experts are working on this as you read this book (well, maybe not if you're reading it at one am, but you know what I mean…). The people who set the exams and the course syllabuses make sure that there is no obvious bias in terms of structure of the content or the wording of the questions. There should be no such thing as 'a girl's subject' or 'a boy's subject', yet there is a marked imbalance in certain subjects. Just look around your own classes.

HOW TO PASS SQA EXAMS

I don't want to be accused of biased thinking, but research suggests:

Girls

◆ favour working alone, but are happy to share ideas with friends

◆ place great importance on reading and thinking

◆ tend to listen carefully to advice and follow instructions

◆ are capable of multitasking (working on several tasks at the same time)

◆ tend not to take risks and try to be logical about the tasks in front

Boys

◆ tend to be greater risk takers and often charge straight into a task without thinking it through

◆ need early success or may be more likely to give up

◆ tend to be more competitive, challenging and loud in their studies

◆ tend to be stronger at solving problems and visual tasks

Once again, an internet search will provide lots of data on this topic.

Reflection Time

Think back on the last few pages. So what type of learner are you? How are you going to compensate for some gaps in your style of learning?

Multiple intelligence and emotional intelligence

We now know a lot more about the workings of the brain. As has been shown above we can recognise that people tend to favour one side of the brain more than the other. So are you intelligent?

It is thought that we can show our intelligence in more than one way, although we may have to work harder at recognising our less strong areas. An American called Howard Gardner developed a theory, and according to him there were seven (but now eight, or even nine!) different styles of intelligence, also known as multiple intelligences. What amazing creatures we are!

The core seven:

◆ mathematical (the questioner)

◆ linguistic (the word player)

◆ visual (the visualiser)

◆ kinaesthetic (the body mover)

◆ interpersonal (the socialiser)

◆ intrapersonal (the loner)

◆ musical (the music lover)

And the extra two:

◆ emotional (awareness of others and their needs)

◆ naturalistic (nature lover)

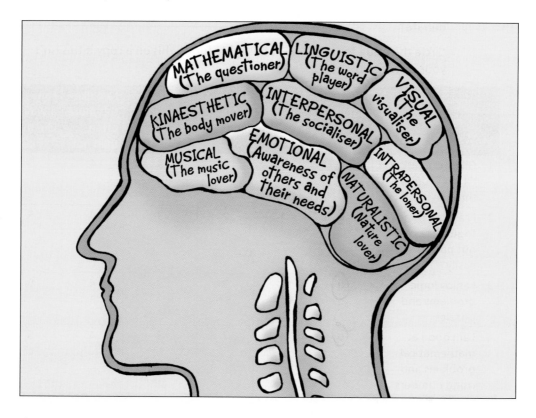

There are several sites online where you can be guided to work out your preferred learning style. Try a search on 'learning styles'. The BBC site 'ready to learn' is also good: www.bbc.co.uk/learning

Questions *and* Answers

SAQ 3 Fancy a quick shot at recognising where you fit in the multiple intelligence debate?

Circle the value for each line in this table (or do this on a copy if this isn't your own book).

	This is not like me at all	I am rarely like this	This is a bit like me	This is sometimes like me	I am like this more often than not	I am always like this
1 Give me a task and I'll work logically through it	0	(1)	2	3	4	5
2 I can link things together and pick out patterns easily	(0)	1	2	3	4	5
3 I enjoy logic problems and puzzles	(0)	1	2	3	4	5
4 I am good at mathematical problems and using numbers	(0)	1	2	3	4	5
Mathematical scores						
5 I can picture scenes in my head when I remember things	0	1	2	3	4	(5)
6 I am good at reading a map	(0)	1	2	3	4	5
7 I am observant. I often see things that others miss	0	1	(2)	3	4	5
8 I like mind maps, charts and diagrams	0	(1)	2	3	4	5
Visual scores						
9 I can sort out arguments between friends	0	1	(2)	3	4	5
10 I like to work with a team	0	1	(2)	3	4	5

Questions and Answers continued

	This is not like me at all	I am rarely like this	This is a bit like me	This is sometimes like me	I am like this more often than not	I am always like this
11 I enjoy social events, like parties	0	1	2	3	(4)	5
12 I am interested in why people do the things that they do	0	1	2	(3)	4	5
Interpersonal scores						
13 My mood changes when I listen to music	0	1	2	3	(4)	5
14 I can pick out different instruments when I listen to a piece of music	0	1	2	3	4	(5)
15 I enjoy making music	0	1	2	(3)	4	5
16 I can remember pieces of music easily	0	(1)	2	3	4	5
Musical scores						
17 I am good at controlling my moods and behaviour	0	1	(2)	3	4	5
18 I am self motivated and set my own targets	0	(1)	2	3	4	5
19 I often set goals for myself or make plans for the future	0	1	2	(3)	4	5
20 I often find myself dreaming or lost in my imagination	0	1	2	3	4	(5)
Intrapersonal scores						

Questions and **Answers** continued

	This is not like me at all	I am rarely like this	This is a bit like me	This is sometimes like me	I am like this more often than not	I am always like this
21 I am good at explaining things to others	0	1	②	3	4	5
22 I really enjoy a good argument	⓪	1	2	3	4	5
23 I can use lots of different words to express myself	0	①	2	3	4	5
24 I enjoy writing stories	0	1	2	3	4	⑤
Linguistic scores						
25 I like to work with my hands	0	①	2	3	4	5
26 I enjoy physical activity	⓪	1	2	3	4	5
27 I have a good sense of balance and like to move around a lot	0	①	2	3	4	5
28 I cannot sit still for long	⓪	1	2	3	4	5
Kinaesthetic scores						
29 I like or keep pets	0	1	②	3	4	5
30 Pollution makes me angry	0	1	2	3	④	5
31 I can recognise and name different birds, trees and plants	⓪	1	2	3	4	5
32 I enjoy being out in the open air	0	1	2	③	4	5
Naturalistic scores						

Questions and Answers continued

SAQ 4 So where do you think your strengths lie? Note down your scores from the table.

Group 1 Mathematical:

Group 2 Visual:

Group 3 Interpersonal:

Group 4 Musical:

Group 5 (Intrapersonal:

Group 6 Linguistic:

Group 7 Kinaesthetic:

Group 8 Naturalistic:

SAQ 5 Now plot your scores on the following chart and shade in the sectors.

It is of course possible to have high scores (15+) on more than one 'intelligence style'.

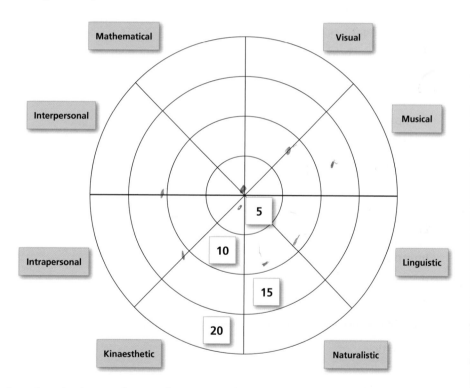

So, what do the results say about you? This quiz gives you an idea of what your current thinking style or styles are. Remember, that the brain is very adaptable, and you should be able to improve your performance in any one of these categories with practice.

SAQ 6 Make a list of the subjects you are currently studying. Make another list of the skills required for that subject and link the skills to the eight (or nine) styles of intelligence. You will probably find that you really require a whole range of styles of thinking. So how can you improve? Have a look at the following summary tips. Add some more yourself.

How to study in a 'multiple intelligence' way

Mathematical

◆ ask why and how

◆ seek to explain the topic step-by-step in detail

◆ experiment

◆ play mathematical games e.g. suduko

Example of such thinkers: Newton, Archimedes, Einstein

Visual

◆ draw sketches and mind maps

◆ visualise the topic in your mind

◆ cover the wall in 'post it' notes

Examples of such thinkers: Hirst, JK Rowling

Interpersonal

◆ form a self help study group

◆ teach it to a friend

◆ recognise and value differences between people

Examples of such thinkers: Churchill, Mandela

Musical

◆ look for links between music and emotions

◆ sing it to yourself

◆ look for sensitivity between words, meanings and music

Examples of such thinkers: Lennon, McCartney, Mozart

Intrapersonal

◆ ask yourself the importance of what you are learning

◆ stop and reflect what you have done

Examples of such thinkers: Freud, Foucault

Linguistic

◆ take detailed notes

◆ make a list or checklist

◆ explain it to someone else

◆ read and read

Examples of such thinkers: Keats, Martin Luther King, Shakespeare

Kinaesthetic

◆ mime or dramatise your work

◆ write keywords out in large letter on sheets of paper

◆ practise the skill or game

Examples of such thinkers: Beckham!

Naturalistic

◆ look for patterns of life

◆ consider how the information fits into your natural life

Examples of such thinkers: Darwin, David Attenborough

Your memory has a natural rhythm. (Let's hope it doesn't beat in time to some of that strange electronic stuff!) At the end of an hour's studying, your mind absorbs the information you have just studied so that the ability to recall rises, peaks after ten minutes and then starts to fall! Reassuring!

If you attended a class on the periodic table on a Friday, and then threw your notes into a deep hole in your room then how much would you remember by Monday morning? Well the experts would tell us that you will have forgotten 80 per cent of what you had learned. Depressing!

So what can you do about it?

Study for as long as you can manage, but make sure that you work in chunks of time (30 to 50 minutes) with a break of ten minutes, where you relax or do something physical. Then review what you have learned:

◆ ten minutes after learning

◆ one day after learning

◆ one week after learning

◆ one month after learning

◆ six months after learning

You will notice that this dramatically changes the time you can recall information.

Emotional intelligence

This is the 'hot topic' for latest research into learning approaches. Sitting on my desk is one of those calendars with a rip off section that has a witty saying for every day of the year. On the day I wrote these words, the day's message was: 'the brain is a wonderful organ. It starts working the moment you get up in the morning, and stops working the moment you get into work.'

Daniel Goleman coined the term, 'emotional intelligence', and describes it as 'a different way of being smart'. To be this, we need to be aware of ourselves and use our own feelings when we are making decisions and learning something new. If you have this awareness, then Goleman says that you will be a better learner or manager, being more motivated and in better control of your actions. So are you 'emotionally intelligent'?

Emotional intelligence is also about your values in life. The guidelines by which you wish to lead your life, those things that to you are right, not wrong and good, not bad. These values guide you through life, including how you will approach studying.

Activities

Another self-evaluation!

Score yourself out of ten (meaning total agreement) and one (the opposite end of the scale) on each of the following statements.

◆ Are you a positive person?

◆ Do you care about how other people are doing and feeling?

◆ Are you pretty much in control of your actions?

◆ Do you show empathy (compassion) for others when they are in a mess?

◆ Do you cooperate with others?

◆ Are you able to spot when someone is upset or lost or lonely?

◆ Do you listen, think, then act?

◆ Can you respect that others may have views different from yours?

◆ Can handle emotions and impulses, such as anger?

◆ Can you evaluate your own strengths and weaknesses?

So, do you value hard work, care for others, stay healthy and try to be a good friend? If yes, you are on the way to being emotionally intelligent. Goleman says that this will enable you to be more confident and motivated, more effective in your relationships, friendships and education.

If you scored 100 then you are on the way to being classified as a 'living saint'! Anything over 60 is good. But if you are convinced with the theory, then look for ways to improve your own 'emotional intelligence'.

Summary

In reflection, what has this section come up with?

You have a learning style. This is made up of several linked issues, some you have little control over (structural) and some unique to you (agency). You have been introduced to right/left hemisphere thinking, the VAK learning approach, to multiple and emotional intelligences as well as some gender traits.

Memory games

Of course you do not pass an exam using memory alone. As you know, there are many other key skills to get a hold of. However it does you no harm to consider ways to improve your memory.

I remember watching Derren Brown on the TV and was amazed at his memory. Had he really memorised the Glasgow telephone directory? There are a number of techniques generally recognised as having a positive impact on your memory. Since it was obvious that he had not memorised it, either he was cheating or it was pure 'magic'! I have read his book on memory improvement (in fact I wanted to quote something from it, but at the moment I can't remember where I put it...) and he suggests some simple easy techniques. Here is a sample of some memory techniques.

Synaesthesia

This, as shown by research, is the linking of memory with our senses. When you want to remember something pleasurable, link it with a nice smell or sound, taste or smell!

Landmarks

People recall where they were doing at the time of shocking news. I can remember what I was doing when I heard the news of the death of Michael Jackson (in a bar) or Princess Diana (driving off at the first hole of the golf club, got a six...) We associate the emotional, shocking, silly, funny, embarrassing or outrageous with what and where we were at a particular time.

Peg system

This is a great way to remember numbers. All you do is give each number a 'peg' word and then make up a silly story about it with the words in the correct order. For example: 528901

5 = dive, 2 = blue, 8 = gate, 9 = wine, 0 = nemo (zero!), 1 = sun

So, I dive into the blue water, sit on the gate and have a glass of wine as Nemo swims by looking up at the sun!

> **Question**
>
> **SAQ 7** Go on, try 359271!
>
> Mind you I'm not convinced that I can think of any occasion when I have used this technique!

Rhymes

This works in the same way as the 'peg' system, only here you try to make up and remember a little rhyming poem. I am sure that when you try to figure out the number of days in the Month of April, you start to recite the little poem, '30 days has September, April, June and November...' There you are. Problem solved.

Mnemonics

A mnemonic (sounds like nim-awn-ic when you say it) is a simple way of helping you to learn lists. This is a really useful technique for fact based subjects such as geography or biology. When you have sequence to remember or a list of features to describe, then you can take the first letter of all the names and make up a sentence. Sometimes the crazier that sentence, the easier it to jog the memory and surprisingly enough, you can remember the detail!

For example, those of you who know your biology will be aware that there are seven characteristics of living organisms. Mr Grief is the mnemonic to use to remember them: movement, reproduction, growth, respiration, irritability, excretion and feeding. Get it!

In geography you can use this technique to remember the difference between stalagmites and stalactites. Stala**g**mites grow up from the **g**round, stala**c**tites grow down from the **c**eiling.

Another example would be if we needed to learn the names of the planets in our solar system going from the star in the middle (the Sun) out into space. We take the first letters of the planets in the correct order and use them to make up a sentence using other words. It helps if these sentences are funny or make great sense.

Planets	Sample mnemonic	Your mnemonic
Mercury	My	
Venus	Very	
Earth	Easy	
Mars	Method	
Jupiter	Just	
Saturn	Stores	
Uranus	Up	
Neptune	Names	

Name game

This is an idea for remembering names which is useful, for example, in English literature or for trying to remember quotes or names in history. My old history teacher was called Mr Campbell. So using this technique how do you remember this name? You are already there! He is camping on the side of a hill! Try out a variety of names from your studies, e.g. oxbow lake.

This technique works because you have to use both sides of the brain. The left side holds the name, and the right brain remembers the silly image. Together they help you recall.

Repetition

When I learn something new, that data goes into my short term memory file. This is a holding area for new information and, unless I move it out, it will quickly be replaced with newer stuff. So, how do I do this? Repetition is one of the best ways. You can tell it to someone else, write it down, or repeat it in our head.

Reflection Time

This has been a long and demanding chapter. Spend some moments flicking back through it and attempt some of note taking and remembering skills that have been introduced.

After you've done that, the next chapter gives you some more background information that is specific to SQA examinations. It may not help you in specific study methods, but it should once again help to reassure you about the processes that go into preparing and marking your examinations (and your appeals, if you need them, but I hope you don't…).

YOUR SQA EXAMS – THE INSIDE STORY

If you're sitting SQA exams, only two dates really matter to you: the day of the exam and the day the results come out.

What you probably don't realise is how much work is done by exam teams and SQA staff for a long time before the exam takes place – and even for a couple of months after the results come out. And why does it take three months to get the results out anyway?

Admittedly, knowing this won't improve your grade, but perhaps you'll be reassured to know how much effort is taken to make your exam fair and your result accurate. Please note, all subjects will differ, and the Appeals procedure may vary slightly each year, but the following pages offer an overview of the procedures common to most exams.

Stage 1: Preparing the exam paper

The question paper that appears on your desk on a day in May will have started its life over two years earlier. At that stage, the Principal Assessor and the setters begin drafting the question paper and revising it during a series of meetings until they are satisfied that they have a paper which is:

◆ in line with the course arrangements

◆ broadly similar to previous exams

◆ challenging enough to distinguish A, B and C performance

◆ most important of all, fair

Before the end of the year (we're still 18 months away from the date this exam will be sat by candidates), the paper has to be 'vetted'. This involves three outside experts (vetters) who have wide experience in the subject. They meet with the Principal Assessor and setters to go through the question paper in detail. The vetters will point out any deviation from the course arrangements and any unclear or ambiguous wording. They will ensure that the exam is fair. They will also look out for any breaches of SQA guidelines about race, gender and taste. In addition, the marking instructions which will be used to mark the papers after the exam are checked and approved by the vetters. When the 'vetted draft' is agreed, the paper is ready to be typeset.

As a final check, the paper is then sent to the scrutineer, another independent subject expert, whose task is to work through the paper to ensure it can be completed in the time available and that calculations and problems given in, for example, maths, physics and business management papers can actually be solved.

A final proof check is now carried out by the Principal Assessor, the Qualifications Manager, and staff at SQA's Question Paper Unit. The paper is now ready for use on the exam date which is still over a year later – although it is available as a 'contingency paper' for the current year in the event of any unexpected problem, such as a breach of security.

The printed question papers are distributed to Chief Invigilators ready for use on the day of the exam, when candidates the length and breadth of the country open them up at exactly the same time and write their answers in the time permitted. This means it's time to start…

Stage 2: Marking the exam

The description that follows is of the traditional 'home' marking, which is used for most exams. There are, however, some alternative models, such as Central Marking, where all the markers are together for several days in the one venue, and SQA is beginning to introduce some online marking methods too.

After you leave the exam room, your exam scripts are gathered in by the invigilators and organised into bundles of ten (alphabetically, according to pre-printed forms sent out by SQA). They are then put into envelopes (always referred to as 'packets') with computer-coded labels, and sent in a sealed bag to SQA in Dalkeith. When the packets arrive, they are 'scanned in' to the central computer system so that the packet's whereabouts are always known, but they are not opened. All the packets from all the centres are then divided up among the markers who have been appointed to mark the exam that year. No marker is ever sent more than one packet from the same school or college.

Each marker's 'allocation' is then sent to her or his home address (never to a school or college) along with copies of the exam paper and the draft marking instructions. However, they can't start marking yet, because they will have to attend a markers' meeting first. They are asked to spend the days before the meeting looking at the draft marking instructions and some of the scripts in their allocation to see if the instructions are going to cover all the answers given by candidates.

Between the day of the exam and the day of the markers' meeting, the exam team carry out their preparation for the meeting. What happens in most subjects is that samples are chosen from the scripts as they arrive at Dalkeith and are photocopied for use at the Meeting. Copies ('photostats') are sent to all markers to study before the meeting, and the exam team discuss them over the next few days and iron out any problems with the marking instructions.

On the day of the meeting, all the markers gather in a central location for a day and discuss with the exam team how the exam is going to be marked. For bigger exams, this can mean well over 100 people travelling from all over Scotland. Attendance is essential: anyone who doesn't attend is not allowed to mark and has to send back all their scripts unmarked. By the end of the meeting, all the strategies will have been agreed and the standards will be clearly set – the draft marking instructions will have been 'finalised'.

After this, markers usually have between two and three weeks to mark their allocation of scripts. The exact number varies from subject to subject, but markers don't get much time to themselves during the marking period! The work must be done at home, marking SQA scripts in a school or college is strictly forbidden.

Once the markers have completed their task, the stage is set for...

Stage 3: Checking the marking

As soon as the marking is complete, the exam team meet and begin the procedure called 'marker check'. This involves checking a sample of every marker's work to see that the marking instructions are being applied correctly and that the standards set at the markers' meeting are being adhered to. If they are, then that marker is noted as 'acceptable'. If they are not, then the marker is designated as 'severe' or 'lenient', with a figure to indicate the extent to which she or he is deviating from the correct standard. This information is fed into the computer for use later on. If the exam team find marking which is seriously inaccurate or dangerously inconsistent, then all the scripts from that marker are re-marked by the team.

By the time this has finished (for subjects with high numbers of candidates, it takes several days), all the marks are in the computer, and SQA can go about the business of...

Stage 4: Setting the grade boundaries

The grade boundaries are the number of marks that are needed for students to achieve As, Bs and Cs for that year. This meeting involves the Principal Assessor, a member of SQA's Senior Management, the Qualifications Manager for the subject, and a statistician from SQA's Research Department. They discuss the question paper and how the candidates have performed as reported by markers and examiners. They consider any issues which may have arisen about the exam's level of difficulty and attention is paid to any questions which may not have performed as expected. With all this in mind, the group will agree the minimum mark required for a C, B and A, and for a 1 – all others are then set automatically by the computer.

But remember that some candidates will have had their papers marked by markers who were not found to be 'acceptable' during the marker check meeting, so their total mark at the moment might not be correct. Now that the grade boundaries are known, the computer can easily identify all those whose final grade is 'at risk' from 'severe' or 'lenient' marking, and this can be rectified at...

Stage 5: The review procedure

Once again, the exam team get together, this time to review the marking of some of the scripts marked by markers who were found to be 'severe' or 'lenient'. There isn't time to look at all such scripts, but in fact there is no need to: what matters are the ones where changing the mark is likely to change the candidate's final grade. Just think: if you've had a 'severe' marker and already have an A, there's no need to do anything about it. And if you've had a 'lenient' marker but have already failed, there's no need to take off any more marks. But if one of your papers has been marked by a 'severe' marker, and you're currently one mark below an A, you deserve to have your paper re-marked to see if you should have an A.

Similarly, if one of your papers has been marked by a really severe marker (who might have been designated 'severe 5', meaning that the mark could be as much as 5 marks out) and you've currently got 4 marks below what is needed for a C, then you may well deserve to pass, so your paper will be re-marked to see what the correct mark is.

This process works both ways, though. So if one of your markers was found to be lenient and you're currently sitting on exactly the lowest mark needed for an A, then it's possible you don't really deserve that, and your paper will be re-marked. If the original mark turns out have been too high, then you're no longer going to get an A.

Occasionally it happens (in exams which involve two papers) that one of your markers is lenient and the other is severe to about the same degree. Generally speaking, these are deemed to cancel each other out, so neither paper is dealt with during the review procedure – in other words, both the marks are 'wrong' but the total is right!

The review procedure can seem a bit brutal when it's dealing with lenient marking – it's possible to start the day with a C and end it with a fail, for example. But if you think about it, it's only fair that passes and Grade As are given only to those who deserve them, and not to those who were lucky enough to get a lenient marker. The review process is a valuable safeguard which ensures that in the end everyone gets the same treatment and everyone's final result is as accurate as possible.

Now that 'correct' final marks are in the computer, there is one last check before results are issued: before you can get a course award, you must have passed all internally-assessed units (NABs). If you haven't, you will not get an award, regardless of how well you might have done in the exam.

Now everything is set for…

Stage 6: Results day

On an eagerly-awaited day early in August, over three months since the first exam was sat, results are sent by post (or email or text, if you have registered for this) and for one day in the year there is guaranteed interest in education on TV, radio and in the papers. There are always people ready to complain: if pass rates have gone up, then there's been 'dumbing down' and the country's going to the dogs; if pass rates have stayed the same, then the teachers aren't working hard enough and the country's going to the dogs; if pass rates have gone down, then pupils are lazy wasters and the country is going to the dogs. Don't worry, it's the same every year!

Remember that 'results day' affects not just you and thousands of other candidates, but their parents, grandparents, extended family – not to forget the teachers and lecturers whose class's results can mean a great deal to them.

Within minutes of the results' being issued, phone lines to universities and colleges are buzzing, mostly from those who have achieved the grades they needed, but there are always some who don't do as well as they expected. Fortunately for them, the SQA has a unique system called…

Stage 7: Appeals

Before the exam, every school and college has to submit to SQA an 'estimate' of your grade for each subject. This is useful for a number of reasons, such as absence from the exam through illness or in the event that exam scripts go missing or are accidentally destroyed. However, their most common use comes with appeals: if your grade in the exam falls short of the estimate, you can submit an appeal, or to be accurate your school or college can submit an appeal on your behalf – you aren't allowed to do it yourself.

When an appeal is submitted it must be accompanied by the 'evidence' on which it was based. This is usually a prelim exam, but other suitable evidence can be sent if it is going to show that you were capable of performing well, under exam conditions, the same kinds of task required in the exam.

The exam team get together once again and scrutinise each appeal individually. If the examiner decides that the estimated grade is fully justified, then your grade will be altered to the estimated one – regardless of how badly you did in the exam. At this stage the examiner isn't interested in your exam performance, since submitting an appeal implies that your exam performance was well below what your school or college think you are capable of. Before doing this, however, the examiner must be satisfied that all of the flowing requirements have been met:

- the prelim paper is one which you could not reasonably have seen in advance (such as past SQA papers or old commercially-produced papers)
- the prelim paper is similar to the real exam in terms of difficulty, coverage, layout, etc.
- the marking instructions are suitable
- the marking instructions have been carried out correctly

The majority of appeals are not successful. The most common reasons for an appeal not being granted are:

- the prelim paper doesn't cover the whole course
- the prelim paper is too easy
- the prelim paper has been obviously designed to favour optional topics, subjects, texts, etc. taught in that school or in particular classes
- the marking has been too generous

In other words, nothing is guaranteed. Just because you were told you scored an A in the prelim, you can't expect SQA to give you an A on a plate just for the asking. Schools and colleges are understandably keen to encourage their candidates and boost their confidence, so they will sometimes set a prelim that is not a fair reflection of what you will see on the day and/or mark it very generously. Then when they draw up their estimates they pitch them too high, and it is inevitable that some candidates will not achieve these grades in the real exam. To put it bluntly, if you get a C for an easy prelim, it's not really surprising if you fail the real thing.

Appeals are for cases of 'serious underperformance' and are not designed for those whose estimate was too high in the first place. Perhaps the word 'Estimate' is a bit misleading: a lot of schools assume that you will improve between the prelim and the exam (you probably will) and build this in to their estimate, but SQA insist that they get hard evidence of 'demonstrated attainment', they're not interested in wishful thinking.

Even if the examiner does not award you the school or college's estimate grade, he or she might award a 'partial upgrade'. For example, if you were estimated at A and got a C, the examiner might think that while the evidence didn't merit an A, it was worthy of a B. In addition, as a final check, your exam scripts will be checked for any errors, but these are very rare and, in any case, if you're genuinely worth the estimated grade then the evidence will have demonstrated this, in which case no one needs to bother checking the exam scripts.

So whatever you do, don't rely on an appeal as some kind of guaranteed safety net, despite what your school report card might have said. As you'll see from the preceding pages, the level of attention that is paid by SQA to the quality of the question paper and the accuracy of the marking is vastly greater than any school or college could manage (you wouldn't want to wait three months for your prelim results!), so there's no certainty that your prelim will meet the SQA's demands. The prelim is important, but you need to make sure that you 'do it on the day'.

Stage 8

For you, there is no Stage 8, but it's worth remembering that SQA never sleeps. Appeals (for Standard Grade and Intermediate) aren't finished until the end of October. In November, appointments are made for markers and examiners for next year's exams. In December, the question papers for the year after that are vetted. In January and February, setting begins for

the question papers for the year after that. In March and April, the Folios, Dissertations and Projects start coming in… which takes us to May, when it starts all over again.

Who are these people?

Markers	These are usually practising teachers or lecturers who have applied to SQA to become markers. They must have at least three years' experience of teaching the subject at the level they will be marking. Most will have marked the year before and many will have marked for a number of years. (They are not allowed to mark scripts from their own school or college.)
Examiners	Examiners are chosen from among experienced markers whose marking has been of a high standard for a number of years. Examiners also mark scripts in the same way as markers, and mark both papers if there is more than one.
Setters	Setters are appointed from among experienced examiners who have shown particular interest in constructing exam questions. Like examiners, they mark an allocation of scripts.
Principal Assessor	The Principal Assessor (PA) is the person ultimately responsible for all matters to do with the question paper, marking standards, and supervising all the post-exam procedures. She or he will usually have been a marker, then an examiner, then a setter, and will have a wide experience of all SQA processes. Like an examiner, she or he marks an allocation of scripts.
Exam team	This term covers the PA, the setters, and the examiners. These are the people who come together to carry out all the post-exam procedures: preparing for the markers' meeting; marker check; review; appeals.
Vetters	Vetters are experienced and knowledgeable teachers or lecturers appointed by SQA to check that question papers conform to requirements. Vetters can mark scripts if they wish, but they cannot be part of the exam team.
Scrutineer	The scrutineer is an experienced and knowledgeable teacher or lecturer appointed by SQA to check that question papers are unambiguous, and that calculations etc. are possible.
Qualifications Managers	Qualifications Managers are full-time members of SQA staff. They have responsibility for a subject or group of subjects, and their job is to advise PAs and exam teams, and to ensure that SQA's procedures are correctly carried out for their subject. They have strong subject knowledge and are often former teachers. However, they do not mark or take part in any of the exam team procedures. All decisions are made by the exam team.
Invigilator	Invigilators are appointed to supervise all SQA exams in schools and colleges. They must not be current teachers or lecturers. Only they have access to the question papers (in sealed envelopes) before the exam.

I hope this has been a useful Chapter to explain a little more about how the exam system in Scotland works. It might even have helped you to feel less stressed about your exams, knowing that there is an organisation behind them that consists of real, genuine, human beings!

But just in case you do feel stressed, take a look at the next Chapter…

Chapter 5

DEALING WITH STRESS

Stress affects us all in different ways. Before an exam, some people have to go to the toilet all the time, whilst others don't go for days! A great scholar once said 'It does not matter whether you pass or fail... until you fail!' (I think it was Bart Simpson!)

Stress is good, but too much of it is bad. No one at SQA wants you to be stressed out, and that is why I have emphasised the fairness of the Scottish system.

You may need time to read through this section and to think about the issues raised. We all feel stressed at times in our lives. I do not want to raise this as a major issue if it is something that has not bothered you so far, but you should remember that there is nothing to be ashamed or embarrassed about if you have felt stressed. I personally have suffered from being stressed out. Often people feel that it good to talk to others about this, whether it be a friend, parent or even a doctor.

In the animal world, the response to stress is to run away or to turn and fight ('flight or fight'). Stress can be good, since it increases the levels of hormones flooding through the body and this improves thinking performance. But there is a point where stress levels increase beyond the body's ability to deal with it and performance drops quickly and people face 'burnout'.

Questions and Answers

SAQ 1   So what is stress?

Answer

It is an emotional, mental and physical reaction caused by new or increased pressures, which are greater than our coping resources. Okay, that's the psychobabble, but what does it really mean? Things are piling up and you are unable to work your way down the list. Important things get put off, you make mistakes and you feel lousy.

Stress is real.

HOW TO PASS SQA EXAMS

Questions and *Answers* continued

SAQ 2   So how can I tell if I'm under too much stress?

Answer

As stress begins to take its toll physically, emotionally and on your behaviour, you may notice some of the following symptoms:

Physical reaction	Emotional reaction
breathlessness	aggressive
sweating	fear of the future
cramp	lack of interest
lack of appetite/cravings for food	irritable
feeling sick/dizzy	lack of humour
indigestion	fear of failure/fear
twitches	depressed
pins and needles	behavioural reaction
tired and restless	crying
sleeping problems	unable to decide
	avoidance
	biting nails
	can't concentrate

Question

SAQ 3   So, what is putting you under stress? Think about the sources, and jot down the main things that jump out at you.

- ◆ Have you taken on more than you can cope with?
- ◆ Do you struggle to keep on top of the work?
- ◆ Have you got issues with time management?
- ◆ Are you under pressure from friends and/or parents to perform, and you are worried about letting them down?
- ◆ Are you worried that you may not be 'clever' enough to pass the exam?

Some tips on dealing with stress

If you are under stress, stop what you are doing and apply any of the following:

♦ Stop worrying about the future, think about today. You can influence the future, but stop worrying about things you have no control over.

♦ Ask yourself, what is the worst thing that can happen? It may not be so bad.

♦ Remind yourself that you are hurting your body. Take ten minutes out.

♦ Do not let the trivia get to you. It is trivia!

♦ Laugh at yourself. Make decisions and act on them.

♦ Share your fears with someone close to you, a friend, parent or a teacher/tutor.

♦ Go back to the sources above, and deal with the individual pressures.

Some extra ideas to lessen stress

♦ Cut back on the caffeine (tea, coffee, chocolate, cola and energy drinks). Caffeine seems to increase the levels of the stress hormone epinephrine and raises blood pressure.

♦ Listen to music (no problem there, then!). The key is to choose something that you like and have a personal relationship with, so it could be Mozart or Abba!

♦ Exercise. Even a 20-minute walk produces positive results.

♦ Watch your diet. It seems that certain nutrients are used up more quickly when you are stressed. So nutritionists might advise us to stack up on the B vitamins (for energy and a healthy nervous system, found in fruit, green vegetables, nuts, cereals and eggs) or vitamin C (a support to the immune system, and found in fruit juices and oranges) and some complex carbohydrates (as in oats, pasta, rice and potatoes).

♦ Sleep. The less sleep you get, the more tense you are likely to feel. Do not work into the early hours of the morning. It is far better to go to bed early and get up a little early. Do I honestly expect young people to go to bed early and get up early? It may work for you. Try deep breathing and relaxation techniques.

Reflection Time

The 'emergency stop'!

If you feel a sense of panic due to stress, for example, if your mind goes blank when you are reading over some notes, say sharply to yourself, 'STOP'. Breathe in, hold your breath for a moment then slowly exhale whilst relaxing your hands and shoulders. Pause and repeat, this time relaxing your forehead and jaw. Stay quiet for a minute and then calmly return to the task.

Question

SAQ 4 Make a list of what is worrying you, and then suggest what you can do about it. This is personal and you may not at this stage wish to share it with anyone. Once you have recognised that you may have a problem, then taking these steps will be a major way to helping you work through it.

For Practice

Deep breathing exercise

Try this exercise for five minutes. Give it go every day for a week and see how it helps.

◆ Sit down, or lie on your back. Be comfortable and loosen any tight clothing.

◆ Be aware of your breathing, the rhythm and the speed.

◆ Put one hand over you upper chest and the other below your ribs on your abdomen.

◆ Slowly let your breath flow out.

◆ Gently breathe in, so that you feel your abdomen rise slowly under your hand.

◆ Breathe out again, feeling your abdomen fall and make sure that you exhale a little longer than you inhaled.

◆ Repeat.

For Practice

Simple relaxation technique

Try this exercise for five minutes.

◆ Have a stretch and a yawn. No problem there, then! Relax the arms and shoulders into a natural and comfortable position.

◆ Shake off the tension. Start with the toes. You can shrug, wriggle or shake them. Whatever eases and relaxes you. Move to the feet, ankle, calves, knees, thighs, chest, arms, fingers, neck…

◆ Feel as if you are letting go. Be calm. Now, move to the face. Drop the shoulders, loosen the muscles in your jaw/face/mouth /eyes.

◆ You can now try to add the breathing technique above.

◆ Almost there. Choose your own magical place. No, not the chemistry lab, but a peaceful place, a desert island, a beach, a lake… Imagine that you are there. Stay there for a few minutes.

Summary

What you can do to reduce the stress levels?

◆ Make sure your goals are realistic.

◆ Get yourself organised.

◆ Talk it out with your friends or parent or guidance counsellor, but emphasise the positive, no group moans!

◆ Go through your routine breathing and relaxation exercises.

◆ Eat well and feed the body and mind.

A 'healthy body and a healthy mind!'

Some years ago I was lucky enough to be invited to join a trip to Japan to study their education system. The big government initiative at the time was a 'healthy body and a healthy mind!' I was not convinced at the time that this was the job or responsibility of schools. I have changed my view. I think it is your responsibility to look after yourself, but also recognise the role of schools and your parents. So what are the ingredients of a 'healthy lifestyle'? And how will this help you pass exams? This section will briefly deal with food and exercise.

Food

Skip breakfast, feast on pickled onion crisps, grab a few cans of fizzy juice and get some curry sauce on top of your chips! That's your body sorted out! Don't be so daft. Rubbish in… rubbish out.

Your body needs to grow and develop. You need to fuel it properly, and eating healthy food is where it starts. That does not mean that you cannot have all those unhealthy favourites. You know what to eat. Food affects behaviour. A balanced diet is the central building block.

Vitamins   found in fruit and vegetables, nuts, pulses, eggs, dairy products

Proteins   found in dairy products, meat, fish, eggs, nuts and pulses

Carbohydrates   found in bread, potatoes, cereal and pasta, cakes, biscuits and sweets

Fats, sugar and salt   found almost in everything, especially processed foods crisps, butter, oils, chocolate, 'fast' foods

The government is considering whether to use the 'traffic light' system on foods, and many supermarkets have already introduced such a system on their food packaging. A healthy diet has lots of 'green' traffic light foods. Try to cut back on the 'reds'. We do need fat and sugar (to help provide us with energy) and salt (for body fluids) but if you overdo them then you are storing up problems for later in life.

Eat breakfast. How daft is it to go and sit and exam without fuel in your body? I asked a senior class I had one day, when I was under-whelmed with their responses to my carefully worded and witty questions, how many of them had had breakfast that day. Fewer than half! Think about it and try to 'break the fast' and put fuel into your body. So can you snack? Of course you can, but remember that a snack can include fruit, nuts, raisins, even some chocolate. You will feel better if you eat sensibly and you will have more energy to study.

Water or Vimto? Best to stick to water for the exam. Not drinking enough fluid can give you a headache and reduces concentration. Go easy though, and try not to drink a full three litres just before the exam!

Question ?

SAQ 5   Review your diet and plan some changes.

Remember to take water into the exam, and that there is nothing wrong having a bar of chocolate, nuts or dried fruit to give you some instant energy.

Exercise

Not everyone can be an athlete such as me! Just for your information, I once held the world record for… (You will have to wait until the end of this section to find out more.) I shattered the existing world record on a Saturday afternoon in Renfrewshire, Scotland, watched by dozens of people in the summer of 1982! (If I remember rightly, I had a good breakfast that day…)

You either take part in sport or you don't. I can't imagine that you are going to change much at this moment. You can follow more individual pursuits such as swimming, cycling, walking or even running. Or you might need the presence of others to get you going, such as in football or aerobics. My advice is to continue what you do, build it into your planning programme, and if possible for those of you who don't do much, start walking a little more.

I have written the ultimate diet and health book: 'The Geddes Plan'. I am going to share the entire contents of the book with you for absolutely nothing… here it is.

'Eat less, walk more'.

When you are stressed, there is a surge of adrenalin which is 'bottled up' because of anxiety. Physical exercise is one way in which you can release adrenalin. A brisk walk or swim will release stress and let you move calmly back into your study. Build time for pleasure into your life. Hard work must be balanced with fun.

Question

SAQ 6   Review your level or exercise and plan some changes.

Sleep

Stress can disturb sleep patterns, leaving you tired and ineffective. Make space to unwind at bedtime. Listen to relaxing music. Imagine yourself parcelling up your worries and locking them away for the night.

Negative thoughts

Many people constantly tell themselves that they are unlikely to succeed in life. These pessimistic messages can come from early childhood, but they impact negatively on our learning as young adults. We need to consciously tell ourselves that we will cope with study if we apply all the advice given in a book such as this. Try to avoid group negativity when you and your friends all get together for a depressing group moan. It does not do you any good!

Remember

◆ Exams are not designed to catch you out, they are an opportunity for you to demonstrate your abilities.

◆ Examiners like giving marks to people who do what is asked of them.

◆ Exams can be completed in the allocated time.

◆ Everyone's memory is sufficient.

Believe it or not, the world record mentioned a few pages ago was for 'hurling the haggis'. For this true test of athleticism and manhood, I stood on a whisky barrel and threw a deep frozen haggis over 40 metres, the first person ever to have done so! I guess you are thinking… 'respect'!

Chapter 6

THE EXAM APPROACHES

The big day has arrived. The early morning visit to the toilet has been negotiated!

So you've done the work, studied hard, and know that you should do well. However, there are still some techniques that you can use to fail at the last moment! So how can you now throw it all away?

Question

SAQ 1   True or false?

1   Exam questions are carefully worded to catch you out.

2   Examiners are very mean with their marks.

3   Exams are nothing more than a test of memory, so they favour those that remember things easily.

4   You only do well if you can think fast and write quickly.

5   Exams are dangerous to your health since they get you stressed.

Answer

All five statements are false. As you will have seen from Chapter 4, great consideration is given to the wording of questions, all work is marked to the same standard and there is an appeal system which favours you, the hard working student.

As I said at the start of this guide, passing an exam is 35 per cent knowledge, 35 per cent luck and 40 per cent knowing how to pass an exam (don't forget of course the crucial two per cent for the good breakfast!).

Of course, it is not really that at all. It is probably 50 per cent course knowledge and 50 per cent exam technique. I am convinced that technique is this important. It is vital to stay cool, confident and calm throughout:

◆   You must take time to read the exam paper and select the best questions.

◆   You must manage your time so that you can complete all the questions.

◆   You must answer the exact wording of the question (called the rubric of the question).

◆   If you have revised thoroughly then the techniques can be learnt quickly and applied with a little thought.

SQA exams aim to test your understanding. They have questions worded in a particular way to make sure that you have this broad understanding. However, you need to be very careful that you answer the exact question set.

Examiners are normal people! Most have been teachers and understand what you are going through. They take a delight in students doing well. However, since they often have hundreds of papers to mark in a short time, it is best to make it easy for them to award you marks. Make sure your answers are relevant, well structured and clearly written.

A few years ago a couple of my students turned up at the right location at the correct time of the day. The trouble was that they were precisely 24 hours late! So, you do not need to be a genius to work out the following:

◆ Make sure you know the exact location, time and date of each exam. Arrive early. However, it is best to avoid talking to others, it can become depressing.

◆ Have all the necessary equipment with you. Take spares. Avoid the last minute panic by getting out the kit in the days before the exams. Some people like to write up a check list of what they need to take to each exam.

◆ Remember your candidate number.

◆ If you read the section above on relaxation techniques, try to find a quiet spot and try out a breathing exercise. It works for me.

◆ Eat breakfast. Take water. Do you need tissues? Nothing worse than your nose dripping for two hours over your French answers! Even take along your lucky charm!

◆ Listen carefully for final announcements. There may be a correction to a question.

◆ Read the question booklet. Nearly every year someone tries answering every English essay title. (It is not easy writing 25 essays in 1½ hours instead of just the one that is required!)

◆ Take a watch.

◆ It is best to work out beforehand how much time you can spend on each section. You must be rigorous about this. However make sure you leave time to check everything and, do NOT leave the examination room early. SQA makes every effort to allocate fair and reasonable time for all their exams (see Chapter 4 again).

◆ Expect to panic. But only for a moment! Now settle yourself down and look at the questions again. Take time to read through the full paper. If the exam allows a choice of section or question, take time to think about the one(s) you are going to do.

◆ Remember one way to guarantee a poor mark in any section is to answer a different question to the one that they have actually asked you to do! Some lengthy questions involve a fair amount of writing. Jot down some planning notes. Separate the thinking bit from the physical chore of writing.

◆ Link the length of your answer with the number of marks awarded! A question for two marks does not require 15 lines of writing! Use a ruler or a pencil or whatever. Remember that markers love to see students attempting little diagrams or sketches. Make sure that they have a heading and are labelled as fully as you can.

◆ Leave space at the end of each question. You can come back to any question later.

◆ Stick to your plan. This strategy should have developed from your revision and preparation. You know which topics to cover and the amount of time you will have for each part of the paper.

◆ Cross out anything that you do not want the marker to read.

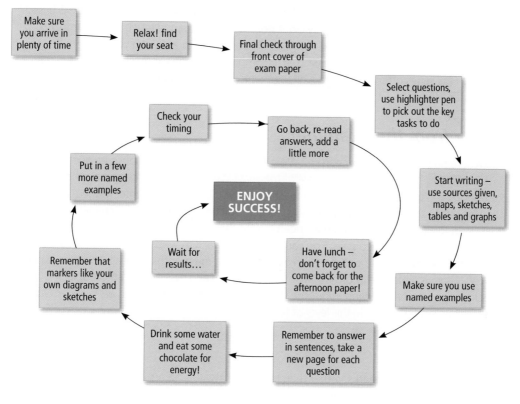

SAQ 2 Make a list with four reasons why you should pass the exam.

Top Tip

Tell yourself:

I am in control and I can cope with the exam.
I've done everything possible to ensure I will pass. I will pass.
I will not concern myself with others.
I have the skills and techniques to pass.
I deserve to pass!

After the exam

Beware of post exam analysis, don't compare your answers. The more you talk about the exam, the more confused and 'cheesed off' you are likely to become. Don't panic. You won't be the only student anxious about the answers. Have some fresh air and food. Take time to relax (even if the next exam is tomorrow!). After a break, focus on the next exam and reflect on how you might improve your exam technique.

You cannot change the past. Look forward. Think positive!

SQA course syllabuses outline exactly what you need to know, and the examination is based on the syllabus. Exams are fair. The syllabus does not really change much from year to year and, if it has changed, teachers are always well informed with at least a year to plan. Unfortunately the syllabus is often written in complex language for teachers. Books in the *How to Pass* series often break down all the themes and topics into small achievable and understandable bits.

View from the examiner

So where do these exams come from? What fiendish mind dreams up obscure questions to fail you? What do these people do the rest of the year? Well, of course, the people who set the questions and papers are experienced teachers. As you've seen in Chapter 4, there are checks at every stage to make sure that you, the student, will be fairly treated. The papers are designed to allow students who have been taught the course and have a broad understanding of the content and skills, to pass. You can even go to the SQA website and download the Principal Examiner's comments for each examination some months after all results have been issued. There is a mass of information about the system and every exam and course. It is fascinating each year, reading about the strengths and the weaknesses of each paper. Not many exam systems provide this level of feedback.

Markers

Their job is to give you marks, rather than take them away. Markers generally allocate according to the three key criteria:

◆ Presentation

◆ Structure

◆ Content

I asked a group of SQA markers from a range of subjects to list the reasons why students fail.

This is what they came up with:

◆ Failure to follow the basic examination instructions; e.g. about the number of questions to answer from each section of the paper.

◆ Misallocation of time, at worst resulting in insufficient questions being answered.

◆ Failure to answer the question set, misreading or misinterpreting the question e.g. being asked to 'explain', but the answer only 'describes'.

◆ Poorly presented answers, e.g. lack of planning leading to weakly structured, disorganised answers.

◆ Writing illegibly.

I've marked my share of exam papers over the years. So why do we do it? I could say it was to gain inside experience of the system or being able to pass on tips to my students. Possibly it was the cheque that arrived just in time for the summer holiday!

So write as legibly as you can. Take some care over this. Buy a decent pen. Only use black or blue ink. Green and red ink is not acceptable. Cheap pens blot and the final product looks lousy. I know that you have already got a writing style, but practise writing fairly quickly and don't write at a size that is either too small or large. In most subjects, markers love to see evidence of planning. And does spelling matter? Of course it does, but if you leave sometime to read over your answer you will pick up the bulk of the little errors that can creep in when you are getting tired. The examiner is not interested in whether you can just memorise facts and you are unlikely to get a question which says, 'write everything you know about…'

Below is a list of verbs (or the action words) used in exam papers and an explanation of what you are expected to do:

Account for   Explain why something is the way it is.

Analyse   Work out in some detail what is being presented to you.

Annotate   Add information to a diagram or sketch.

Argue   Make a case for and/or against a viewpoint and back it with evidence.

Assess   Use your judgement to come to a conclusion on the strength of the facts.

Compare   Identify similarities and differences between two or more things. Draw up distinction between options. Evaluate.

Contrast   Point out the differences. Draw up distinction between options. Evaluate.

Describe   Give an 'in depth' account.

Discuss   Debate. Give examples. Talk about.

Explain   Show why something is the way it is. Give a reason.

Identify   Name. Clarify. Pick out the key features.

Illustrate   Show something with examples.

Justify   Show your reasons.

Outline   Give a summary.

Review   Make an overall assessment.

Suggest   More than naming. Give ideas. Advise on course of action.

Summarise   State the key points.

Feng Shui and studying – is there anything in it?

There are many books and websites that offer far more detailed guidance on Feng Shui, and this book can only give the topic brief mention. Feng Shui is the ancient Chinese practice of spatial arrangement to create the most harmonious and lucky surroundings in our living and work places. It teaches us how to arrange our study area and gives guidance on the best way to lay out furniture, the use of lighting and the careful use of colour.

The Chinese view of the universe relies on the balance of 'yin' and 'yang' forces, as well as the productive and destructive cycles of the five elements (earth, fire, metal, wood and water). It is based on the central concept of the life forces which exist in the atmosphere, and the importance that our living space is in balance. The idea is that getting Feng Shui right brings good fortune.

Many people find Feng Shui guidelines helpful in study, and others think that they are nonsense. As ever, what works for some people might not work for others. To the Chinese, success in education and exams is viewed as the first vital step in carving out a substantial life and career. And, of course, to follow Feng Shui guidelines alone does not bring success, but the guidelines say that your efforts will pay off and hard work will show reward.

If you follow Feng Shui, yang energy brings warmth. Rooms should be bright, airy and filled with life. This can be achieved using sounds, bright colours and pictures. Yin is darkness, night, cold and stillness. To enjoy good Feng Shui, rooms should have a mix or balance of both the yin and the yang. Without the coldness of yin, you cannot have the warmth of yang. Rooms that are too dark and quiet (yin) do not have sufficient life energy.

For maximum fortune, your study area should be in the north east section of your room. You should not place plants or flowers in this sector, nor metal objects such as wind chimes or bells. You should place a piece of rock such as a quartz crystal or a clay pot or glass ball here instead. Obviously have some gentle lighting and using the colour red is ideal (but not to excess). Open windows, you need to allow the air to clear and keep the energies fresh.

Whether such guidelines appeal to you or not, it is certainly worth ensuring that your study area is fit for purpose, and helps you to study effectively.

Almost at the end!

I have just been watching a programme on the Discovery Channel by Bear Grylls, ex-SAS member and survival expert. He filmed the programme in the Sahara Desert and survived there by pulling out the intestines from a camel, finding fluid to drink in the stomach, skinning it to make a blanket, frying camel meat on a fire made from camel dung and seeking shelter from the sun inside the rib cage of the beast. (By the way it is already dead!)

Granted, Bear Grylls is unusual. However, he can still teach us priorities for survival in less hostile environments, such as for passing exams. His priorities are:

◆ Do not panic. Don't do anything to make matters worse.

◆ Maintain energy. Eat and drink when you can.

◆ Objectively review the situation regularly.

◆ Avoid denial.

◆ Be an optimist – see hope not hopelessness.

◆ Rejoice that you are alive (and not the opposite!).

◆ Value your strengths. Recognise your weaknesses.

◆ Have courage.

So there you are. Not only have I given you advice to overcome all barriers regarding exams, I have given you the skills to survive in the Sahara!

TIPS FOR PARENTS

Let your parents read this section (after all, they may well have bought the book!).

There is an old expression which says, 'it's a day's work getting started'. So how do you help your son/daughter to get started?

Your interest and involvement can spark enthusiasm in your child and teach them one of the most important lessons in life: that learning can be fun, that it is important and well worth the effort and ultimately rewarding. A little coaching and encouraging throughout the year is important. Don't just leave this until the last few weeks.

Find them space. It is important to have a desk or table where books and materials can be left out. It is so much easier to start if all you have to do is sit down and get on with it.

Your son/daughter will not appreciate you hanging over their shoulder all the time, so it is worth remembering that you need to be discrete in your support. Often they will be grumpy (so what's new, they are 'teenagers' after all). So it is important to set the scene, help create the space and remove distractions. Recognise the difference between 'support' and 'nagging'.

Feed them, give them something to drink, respect their space and take the pressure of them by covering some other chores (e.g. washing the dishes! Mind you, they probably never did this in the first place...)

Make sure the TV is off and remove phones. Go out and invest some money. A good start was buying this book! Do you need to get other test resources? Make sure that the pencils, pens, paper, glue, stapler, folders... are all to hand.

What about use of the internet? There are some super sites based on content/subjects as well as study skill materials (the BBC Bitesize site www.bbc.co.uk/schools/bitesize/ has specific Scottish revision sections). The problem is, of course, all the distractions in the way. As soon as you have turned your back, have they quickly logged into Facebook?

Most importantly, be available. When you get a chance, read through the rest of this book and see what is expected from your son/daughter when they study.

Give praise and, if possible, sit down and have a chat to review what they have done and what they hope to do next.

So what is the key tip on motivating your child? You make them feel good about themselves. You make them strong emotionally.

Of course as a parent I also bribed my children to do well! I am aware that whilst this may work in the short term, it might not provide long term change. Your children need to take responsibility for their own development. When they leave to go to college or university they will increasingly have to fall back on their own strategies.

Please be careful about making comparisons with other students or siblings. Not everyone can achieve 'A' grades in everything. Where commitment is shown, always give praise – irrespective of the grade – in most cases even modest success should be worthy of praise.

Look out for the symptoms of stress (difficulty in sleeping, loss of appetite, upset stomach) and provide support. Stay calm yourself.

Go to the SQA web at www.sqa.org.uk, and check the system.

Reflection Time

Make a list of four things that you can do now to assist your child.

A final Reflection Time for the student...

Reflection Time

Do you remember this earlier note? And have you changed your approach to study since reading it for the first time?

Do you:

◆ set aside time regularly for homework and thinking about your work?

◆ usually spend time cramming the night before the exam?

◆ believe the more I study the less time I have for my friends and having fun?

◆ study with the TV on?

◆ spend three hours solid at studying, without a break?

When you look back at your notes:

◆ do they seem to be incomplete and messy?

◆ do you think: 'Where are my notes?'

Do you:

◆ re-read all your notes regularly?

◆ have problems remembering all the facts?

◆ fail to remember what you did yesterday, let alone last year?

◆ have no idea what will come up in the test or exam?

◆ think that if 'I only had time, my homework would be better'?

◆ think that you should have scored better or that your teacher is harsh/cruel/doesn't like you?

Reflection Time continued ➤

HOW TO PASS SQA EXAMS

Reflection Time *continued*

Do you:

◆ worry that your mind goes blank in a test?

◆ work best when the fear of failure kicks in?

◆ read slowly and worry that you can't get through all this work?

◆ ask how could you read faster?

◆ know what you want to say, but it never comes out that way on paper?

Summary

Final checklist of possible reasons for poor exam marks:

◆ Not answering the exact question as set.

◆ Failing to recognise the exact terms and words used in the question.

◆ Failing to carry out the precise instructions.

◆ Failing to answer all aspects of the question.

◆ Poor time management.

◆ Failing to match the expected length of the answer in the time set.

◆ Spending too long on one question and not enough on the others.

◆ Failing to weight parts of the answer appropriately.

◆ Failing to realise that one aspect of the question (e.g. explain) may carry more marks than another (e.g. describe).

◆ Failing to provide evidence to support an answer.

◆ Such as not providing case study examples.

◆ Or stating the obvious such as the basics or definitions.

◆ Failing to illustrate an answer as required.

◆ Not including a relevant diagram.

◆ Incomplete or shallow answer.

◆ failing to answer due to lack of knowledge.

◆ Not considering the topic in enough depth.

◆ Waffling.

◆ Illegible handwriting.

◆ Poor English expression.

◆ Lack of structure or logic.

◆ Factual errors or 'howlers'.

◆ Failing to correct obvious mistakes.

This book has addressed these issues. You have come a long way in terms of thinking and planning, revising and passing exams.

I would wish you 'good luck' when you sit your SQA exams, but really, if you've paid attention to the advice in this book, you'll know it's not really a matter of luck – so I'll just offer my very best wishes and encourage you to stay calm, and do your best…

Ian Geddes

CALUM'S TOP TEN TIPS FOR HAPPINESS AND ADVANCEMENT

For very many years I taught beside my good friend Calum. Apart from being a decent teacher, he is very funny and full of ideas. Here are some of his ideas. Be amused by some of them, but believe me: there is research evidence to suggest that there is a factual basis for (almost) every tip…

1   Make cd/mp3 recording of facts, details, tricky formulae/words or notes that you can listen to when you're walking or just sitting.

2   Play recordings of information when you are sleeping. Don't make this the main form of revision, but just another way of reinforcing information through osmosis (the gradual, often unconscious, absorption of knowledge or ideas through continual exposure rather than deliberate learning).

3   Use 'post its' or just stick pieces of paper with important revision points in places around your house (make sure they are places you actually go to…) Some suggestions are:

   ◆   on the ceiling straight above your bed
   ◆   on the end of your bed facing you when you're sitting in it
   ◆   inside the fridge
   ◆   where you hang up your coat/jacket/hoodie (and no, we don't mean the floor)
   ◆   around where you study
   ◆   on the walls/door of the toilet/bathroom, beside the mirror (especially for the boys!)
   ◆   where you pick up the TV remote controls
   ◆   inside drawers you use frequently (pants, at least twice a week)

   Go on, be creative in this one. Find places that are clever, even funny. Why not challenge someone in your house to place a certain number of them around the house (not too many) and check with you after two or three days to see if you have found them all. To prove it, you would have to give the details of what was on each piece of paper.

4   When you revise for a subject wear a particular perfume/aftershave/body spray/deodorant for each subject. Your brain will recognise this smell as part of the memory of that revision (you may wish to spray a small amount into the air as well). On the day of the exam wear the perfume/aftershave/body spray/deodorant that you used when you were studying. You may find that an extra spray onto your wrist will mean that you can put it to your nose during the exam to help trigger the memories of that revision. Some people only put it on their wrist and use it as a trigger. If you have two different exams in a day make sure you wash off the one on the wrist for the first exam and add the perfume for the second one onto the other wrist.

5   In a similar vein I know of a girl who only eats a particular flavour of fruit pastilles for each subject and takes only that flavour with her into the examination. It seems to work for her, although like any other food-related reinforcements and triggers they are not recommended for diabetics or those who would become more worked up about the exams because of the sugar rush and adrenaline!

6   Ever noticed that even people who have great difficulty learning information start singing the words to songs very shortly after the song has been released? Or groups of football supporters can learn significant songs for their club very quickly. For some reason many people seem to be able to learn if they sing or rhyme. So why not make up a song that explains part of your course or key facts... it also helps if you sing it along to a tune you already know. Favourite chart songs work for some people and nursery rhymes for others. Some people like to sing others like to rap. What works for you is the best one for you. It might not just be a song that works for you, try making poems or rhymes.

7   Mnemonics (see page 50): I've always found that the best ones make sense on their own, like a sentence that could be said to someone else and it wouldn't sound odd. Funny ones also work and (don't tell parents/teachers) so do rude ones. This is also true for songs or rhymes. Yes, in fact these ones seem to stay with you longer! So if it works for you, do it (but keep the disgusting ones to yourself)!

8   Repetition does work with facts. Some people may tell you this is not the best way, but believe me it really does work. Do something regularly and your body becomes used to it, eventually it just stays with you and you don't really have to think about it. It's muscle memory for the brain in a sort of way. (Think about it, if you get into trouble regularly for something, someone says the same thing to you time after time, I bet you could repeat the words, even make a joke out of the way that person says it. How is that possible?) Some people actually learn key facts by chanting them.

9   Create a lesson to teach someone else a key fact (maybe a family member or a friend you trust). It is better if the person is not taking that subject and has to be taught by you. At the end ask him/her to tell you what he/she understood about what you were teaching, or whether he/she understood it. Encourage him/her to ask questions to clarify points and then try to explain them better. Don't feel bad if you can't answer some questions just use the resources you have (books, jotters, notes, computers, internet, teachers...) to find out the answers and make the key facts clearer to yourself.

10   What about a t-shirt for your boyfriend or a girlfriend with key facts on them? Creating this on a computer and then ironing them onto the t-shirt, or just writing them on, means that you have had to look up the information, look at it, work out which key facts seem important then write or iron them on. That's revision and re-enforcement. Then stare at each other!

Cal's bonus tip! I have a different approach to all those parents who seem to think that revision is all about being locked up with no contact with the outside world. Yes, you will have to do this and focus solely on your work but you must also have variety and contact with others to release any stresses. So why not make use of contacts in ways which can be helpful. Some of the previous ideas talked about meeting with friends and boyfriends/girlfriends and this can be extended in a variety of ways. Develop a 'community of learning' approach.

The key point to this is not to lie to yourself. Of course there will be times when you need a complete break from study, but use the 'community of learning' idea to help you and not to keep you away from making progress towards success. Get your parents involved. Make arrangements with them so this can all be agreed, times given and make it open and above board.

MSN/Contact forums/Facebook/Bebo and any other social networking site can be used to keep in contact and help each other in your 'community of learning'. Talk over problems, point each other to the answers... Be supportive. A limited time for this type of contact is often good as it helps you to focus on the things that are needed in your studying but also arrange a few minutes more for a chat to relieve stress.

What about using your pages on these sites or the name section on your MSN to put in a key fact, or a number of key facts, and when you are online to your friends you are seeing each others' and helping to re-enforce the facts either by intent or by osmosis?

Thanks Cal!

EXAM HOWLERS

Genuine comments taken from a lifetime marking geography exam papers and jotters:

'You can tell from the graph that Sydney has 1200 wet days a year.'

'The National Parks are owned by the Ministry of Defence, so that their tanks, planes and submarines can use the land for training.'

'The majority of National Parks are owned by owners with a very small majority owned by other people who don't own much.

'A problem in the hot dessert is that there is not any water so there are no rivers or lakes, and crops don't grow. So to survive they have to go fishing.'

'A smaller river that joins a bigger one is called an obituary.'

'Metamorphic rocks have been altered by heat and pleasure'

'Ayrshire and Lanarkshire were once famous for their minefields.'

'Shoppers in the CBD of Irvine are dense.'

'People in Viagra are dying from starvation, disease and plaque.'

'A lot of people catch deceases and die.'

'Some of the major causes of hunger include flood, drought and pets such as locusts.'

'Poe mion's house and cow and browes.' (*I never did find out what this was supposed to be!*)

'It has been measured that trees can break wind for up to 40 metres.'

'Hadrian's wall was built near Hexham so that the tourists could get a good view.'

'We need the rainforest because they hold half the worlds known plant life most of which have not even been discovered yet!'

'We can stop population explotion by using contrusption (e.g. condoms, the pile, etc.)'

'Soil erosion is caused by growing the same crap year after year.'

'Sheep can adapt to the cold hills since they have warm woollies.'

'Japanese still kill whales. We should boyscout their goods.'

'The docklands of Glasgow once had jetties and whorehouses.'

'I wood like to think the Liberians at Ardosan libery for there help in ma project.'

And finally, you know it is worthwhile when you read that...

'My favourit sujict is jogruffy. I would like to thank Mr Geddes for absolutely everything. He is the best teacher ever'.

USEFUL WEBSITES

In no particular order, these were all current at the time of writing, and you are reminded that the publisher is not responsible for the content of third-party websites…

www.infomat.net

www.studygs.net

www.open.ac.uk

www.support4learning.org.uk

www.skoool.co.uk

www.ltscotland.org.uk

www.cambridgestudents.org.uk

www.brain.web-us.com

www.bgfl.org

www.bbc.co.uk/learning

www.leckieandleckie.co.uk

www.sqa.org.uk

www.brightredpublishing.co.uk

www.buzanworld.com

www.scqf.org.uk

www.open.ac.uk/skillsforstudy

www.how-to-study.com

www.bized.co.uk

www.bbc.co.uk/schools/bitesize

www.bbc.co.uk/scotland/brainsmart

And finally, remember that you can see the full range of SQA-endorsed *How to Pass* titles at:

www.hoddereducation.co.uk/Schools/Scottish-Curriculum/How-to-pass.aspx

PHOTOCOPIABLE SUMMARY SHEETS

Over the page you'll find the summary sheets of 'top tips' I mentioned on page 2. These can be legally photocopied in any educational institution that has bought the book, or by any individual who has bought the book. You could try pasting them on to card and sticking them around your bedroom – or any room in the house. The more you see of them, the better!

REVISION TECHNIQUES

◆ Create your personal study space.

◆ Get organised: cards, pens, folders, highlighter pens, notes...

◆ Use relaxation techniques to get you into the mood for revision.

◆ Have the session planned. Use your calendar and priority sheet. Know what to do.

◆ Actively read and write notes.

◆ Use your notes and past papers.

◆ Be creative in revision e.g. use mind maps.

◆ Revise using the SMART approach.

   ◆ specific

   ◆ measurable

   ◆ action-related

   ◆ realistic

   ◆ time-based

◆ Leave your study space organised for the next session.

◆ Take breaks and time out and reflect on the session.

EXAMINATION TECHNIQUES

- Be organised and arrive at the exam hall in plenty of time, with all the equipment needed.

- Make sure that you have eaten and have brought water to drink.

- Follow all instructions and answer the right number of questions from each section.

- Remember relaxation techniques.

- Remember that you have done the work so do not panic, read the question again and stay cool.

- Give thought to the exact wording of the questions and plan out your answers.

- Keep your answer legible and check against the plan.

- Be aware of the time.

- At the end, check all answers and add details.

- Match the length of each answer appropriate for the number of marks on offer.

ENJOY YOUR LEARNING

◆ Remember that you selected what to study! So you should be reasonably interested in your courses.

◆ Having a positive frame of mind: this makes it easier to enjoy yourself.

◆ Have fun by being creative in your revision and note taking.

◆ Study to Music – background music can help you to concentrate.

◆ Plan your study programme and remember to mix studying with a social life.

◆ Revise with a friend.

◆ Take regular breaks.

◆ Imagine the feeling you will have when it is all over and the results come through.

READING

- Establish why you are reading e.g.

    - to gain knowledge and understanding

    - to help you to remember

    - to collect information for a project

    - to gather 'in depth' info

    - to help you pas an exam

- Use the SQ3R method

    - survey/scan

    - question

    - read

    - recall

    - review

- Take regular breaks.

- Try active reading.

- Be cautious when reading 'online'.

- Be critical in your reading e.g.

    - who is writing?

    - what is their point of view?

    - what evidence is being presented?

    - is there bias?

    - are there other perspectives or views?

TIME MANAGEMENT

- Create an efficient working space.

- Work out when you can study.

- Create a 'weekly study planner'. Keep it and make sure it is up to date.

- Create your own regular 'priority form'.

- Always make sure that you take time to file and sort out all notes as soon as possible.

- Organise your social life. Recognise the importance of studying for exams at crucial times

- Always look for opportunities to catch up on work (e.g. lunchtime, on a train journey…).

- Be SMART in your studies.

- Be efficient in your reading and note taking.

- Don't waste time by messing about at school/college.

- Use relaxation techniques and have regular breaks to encourage efficiency.

TAKING NOTES

- Write your own notes in your own words (except useful quotes) and avoid plagiarism.

- Always link your notes with the original sources.

- Date all 'handouts' and file them.

- Work out a strategy for taking notes. Establish why the notes are needed.

- Use a variety of methods such as highlight pens, index cards, 'post it cards'…

- Use IT when possible and appropriate.

- Experiment with visual mindmaps

WEEKLY STUDY PLANNER

Fill in your exam or test times for each week. Check with the SQA website for confirmation of these (www.sqa.org.uk)

Fill in the activities that are already scheduled e.g. class times and sport commitments and then fill in your study times.

Time	Monday	Tuesday	Wednesday	Thursday	Friday	Saturday	Sunday
6–7 am							
7–8							
8–9							
9–10							
10–11							
11–12							
12–1 pm							
1–2							
2–3							
3–4							
4–5							
5–6							
6–7							
7–8							
8–9							
9–10							
10–11							
11–12							